DESIGNING RESPONSIVE CURRICULUM

Planning Lessons That Work

Nancy Frey
Douglas Fisher
Kelly Moore

Rowman & Littlefield Education
Lanham, Maryland • Toronto • Oxford
2005

Published in the United States of America
by Rowman & Littlefield Education
A Division of Rowman & Littlefield Publishers, Inc.
4501 Forbes Boulevard, Suite 200, Lanham, Maryland 20706
www.rowmaneducation.com

PO Box 317
Oxford
OX2 9RU, UK

British Library Cataloguing in Publication Information Available

Library of Congress Cataloging-in-Publication Data

Frey, Nancy, 1959–
  Designing responsive curriculum : planning lessons that work / Nancy Frey,
Douglas Fisher, Kelly Moore.
     p. cm.
  Includes bibliographical references.
  ISBN 1-57886-230-2 (pbk. : alk. paper)
  1. Lesson planning—California—San Diego—Case studies. 2. Education—
Standards—California—San Diego—Case studies. I. Fisher, Douglas, 1965–
II. Moore, Kelly, 1971– III. Title.

LB1027.4.F74 2005
371.3'028—dc22

                                                    2004024577

∞™ The paper used in this publication meets the minimum requirements of
American National Standard for Information Sciences—Permanence of Paper
for Printed Library Materials, ANSI/NISO Z39.48-1992.
Manufactured in the United States of America.

CONTENTS

1 Standards, Expectations, and Essential Questions   1

2 Designing Multiple Formal and Informal Assessments   17

3 Identifying Richly Detailed Source Material   39

4 Designing Interrelated Daily Lessons and Culminating Activities   57

5 Literacy Instruction Across Content Areas   71

6 Effective Grouping for Instruction   95

7 Focusing on Diverse Learners   105

References   123

About the Authors   141

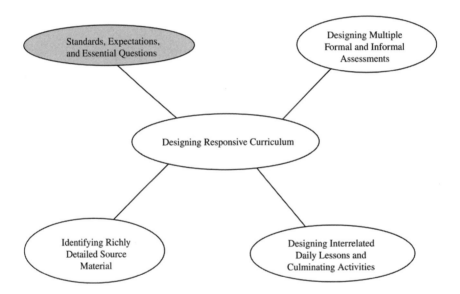

❶

STANDARDS, EXPECTATIONS, AND ESSENTIAL QUESTIONS

Schools are being held accountable for the achievement of all students, not just those who perform well in traditional educational settings. Data on student achievement underscores the evidence of our failure to make best and emerging educational practices available to all urban youth (Meier, 1995; Sautter, 1994). This impact is most significant in large urban communities (U.S. Department of Education, 1996) because urban districts historically have had student dropout rates of over 40%, and over 70% of students read, write, and compute below grade level (Espinosa & Ochoa, 1992). Middle school students who are at risk of dropping out of school are more likely to quit school before ever reaching high school than they are to drop out of high school once they get there (Haberman, 2000).

The fact is, student achievement among urban youth needs to become a national priority. Focusing on the achievement of all youth is logical and justified, but youth in urban environments deserve increased attention. To many people, the problems and needs of urban America seem insurmountable. It is easy to conjure images of massive poverty, dilapidated private and public structures, crime, vandalism, drug and alcohol problems, child abuse and neglect, and gang fights (Atkins, 1994; Zunino & Hill, 2003). Urban and suburban housing and employment patterns continue to result in ethnic and racial segregation and urban unemployment. African American urban males are more likely to die from gunshot wounds than from any other cause. For many, these urban realities become correlated with the fact that over 75% of urban youth are nonwhite, over 150 languages are spoken in these multiethnic communities, over 15% of urban children are limited English proficient, and enormous disparities exist in the educational achievement curves of urban youth. To people who presume causal relationships in these correlations, urban educational reform appears to be pointless and useless. Many of the people who draw such conclusions move if they can, vote for private school voucher initiatives, give up, and, if they do not live there, blame the victims.

Other people, however, look for ways to tap the strength and resilience existing in these urban settings. They know children can hardly be held accountable for their educational failure when little public equity exists, especially when factors such as the size, age, condition, and resources of school buildings; the amount of per student spending; and the degree of tracking are all negatively represented in the inner cities. Many view urban school students' underachievement as a result of the lack of qualified teachers (Howard, 2003). The fact that urban children show no marked differences from others when they enter school and progressively fail in comparison after each year of attendance (Sautter, 1994) turns the attention to school and community structures (i.e., policies and practices) and away from a pessimistic, deficit view of urban children and the expectations held for them (Lee & Burkam, 2003).

People who believe educational reform is possible work hard to bring resources to ideas, ideas to actions, and actions to outcomes. Whether they are involved in building new schools from the ground up with widespread community partnerships or are aggressively challenging traditional tracking, testing, curriculum, or pedagogy, they are demonstrating that change is possible. The reforms that seem most successful in urban settings seem to have a grassroots means of engaging and empowering parents and members of the community to partner with the administrators, teachers, and students of the school.

The teachers whose classrooms we visit in this book are part of the solution. These teachers work in urban environments and focus on a curriculum design process that meets the needs of their diverse student populations. Before we continue, let's take a minute to meet them.

Mr. Tom Giaquinto teaches 20 linguistically and academically diverse kindergarten students. Primary languages spoken in Mr. G's class are Spanish, Vietnamese, Arabic, and English. One student in this kindergarten class receives special support from a speech therapist a few times per week. Mr. G must use effective second-language teaching strategies as he models, scaffolds, and coaches his diverse learners. Mr. G's classroom is saturated with print. Books in baskets line the shelves and rest upon clusters of desks, high-frequency words and students' names fill the word walls, and kid-friendly content standards written in kindergarten handwriting label student work around the room. Mr. G believes that by integrating literacy, movement, and music, his students will be able to make meaning with print in an engaging, comfortable atmosphere.

Ms. Pam Pham-Barron teaches second grade to an equally diverse group of students. In addition to the English-language learners she instructs, Ms. Pham-Barron has one "newcomer" student who immigrated to the United States after school had already begun in September. In order to create a community of learners who interact with one another and take risks in whole- and small-group settings, Ms. Pham-Barron changes her seating arrangements often. Every two months, Ms. Pham-Barron heterogeneously groups her students at clusters of desks to promote many opportunities for partner and small-group discussions. Ms. Pham-Barron team-teaches with the bilingual teacher next door, Ms. Carrie Hultgren. The two teachers integrate their students, giving them opportunities to interact and practice their newly acquired English language skills with one another.

Ms. Aida Allen teaches fifth grade at Rosa Parks Elementary. She has 32 students, all of whom qualify for free or reduced lunch. Ms. Allen has had the rare opportunity to "loop" with her students for six years. She began teaching this group of students in kindergarten and is finishing her final year with them in elementary school in fifth grade. The students in Ms. Allen's class speak Spanish and English. She began instructing these students in Spanish during their kindergarten year and by third grade most of the students were fluent in English. Ms. Allen has five students with special needs in her class. Two students receive support from a resource specialist, two students are supported by a special day teacher, and one student with Down's syndrome is fully included in the classroom. Ms. Allen has always arranged her desks in clusters so students can develop their oral language skills and participate in cooperative group activities.

Ms. Heidi Mellander teaches math at Monroe Clark Middle School. She has 30 to 34 students per period. All of her students qualify for free or reduced lunch and receive sheltered instruction because they are also English-language learners and speak a language in addition to English at home. She teaches as a member of a "house," a group of six teachers who all have the same students. Ms. Mellander enjoys hands-on activities that capture the students' interests. She also works hard to develop a strong rapport with her students, as she knows that many of them are afraid of math.

Mr. Ted Hernandez teaches English and writing to ninth graders at Hoover High School. He is a recent graduate of the San Diego State University's teacher credential program and was hired at the school where he did his student teaching. As in other urban schools, Mr. Hernandez's students qualify for free or reduced lunch and are diverse in terms of ethnicity, exceptionality, and experience with school. Mr. Hernandez loves literature and writing and wants all of his students to love language as well. He knows that the modeling he provides his students is key to their development.

Ms. Maria Grant is a physics teacher at Hoover High School. She believes that students must have authentic experiences with knowledge in order to learn. She structures her class around the state standards and ensures that students have multiple opportunities to engage with ideas. This requires that she plan instruction in such a way as to cycle through ideas several times during the school year. In addition, she knows that classroom organization and management are key. If the students understand the rules and procedures in the classroom, they can focus on learning content.

THE ROLE OF CURRICULUM AND CURRICULUM DESIGN

Curriculum has been described in many ways (Posner, 1995; Trafton, Reys, & Wasman, 2001). Some people talk about curriculum as the content that is covered in a specific class. Others maintain that curriculum is also the set of instructional strategies that teachers use. We use the term *curriculum* to describe a course of study. In other words, we view curriculum as both the content and methods a teacher uses to plan and conduct his or her class. This book focuses on the content of the curriculum and the ways in which teachers ensure that all students access the core curriculum. However, before we can turn to a discussion of responsive curriculum design, we must first examine the standards and expectations that are established for all students.

STANDARDS

The national effort to improve the educational achievement of America's schoolchildren is grounded in the establishment of rigorous learning standards at every level of elementary and secondary education (Roach, 1999). In developing a standards-based system, policymakers and educators hope to refocus teaching and learning on a common understanding of what communities expect students to know and be able to do as a result of their public school experience (Tucker & Codding, 1998). Once established, the standards provide the foundation for deciding what to teach and how to assess students' progress. "At their very best, standards convey our professional vision of good teaching and learning" (Brandt, 2003, p.17).

Curriculum frameworks are outlines that establish benchmarks for curriculum content at the various grade levels, thus providing the broad context from which districts then develop their specific curricula. These benchmarks become the goals and objectives that students should meet in each grade level. In some states, these frameworks merely provide voluntary guidance to local districts as they develop their curriculum. In other states, the frameworks provide the foundation for new statewide assessment systems, as well as guidance for textbook approval, curriculum priorities, and instructional strategies.

The proponents of standards-based reform maintain that if high, rigorous standards are created for all students and clearly communicated to educators, students, family members, business leaders, policymakers, and the community at large, then a coordinated effort can be mounted that focuses on increased achievement (National Association of State Boards of Education [NASBE], 1996; Tucker & Codding, 1998). The intended result is that *all* students—from all socioeconomic backgrounds, and including those with limited English proficiency, and students with disabilities—will achieve (Brandt, 2003; McDonnell & McLaughlin, 1997). In other words, the expectations for all students are increased, and the entire system is focused on helping students achieve those higher expectations.

Types of Standards

Several types of standards are used in schools today. Most commonly, content standards refer to the specific curriculum for a specific class. Often, these are developed at the district or state level. For example, second-grade teachers must instruct students to write clear and coherent sentences and paragraphs that develop a central idea. In addition, a class called "Algebra" has specific competencies that students are expected to master if they are to receive credit in the class. The content standards do not provide teachers with guidance for planning instruction, but do provide teachers with information about what should be taught.

In addition to the content standards, performance standards are often developed at the district or site level to ensure that students can demonstrate their knowledge across traditional academic disciplines. An example of a second-grade performance standard may be to revise written work in order to improve the sequence of events and provide descriptive detail. The Hoover Learner Outcomes (HLOs) listed here are examples of performance standards. If every teacher, from kindergarten through middle school and then high school, understands what students are expected to learn in order to receive a diploma, they can work together as a K–12 team to ensure that all students are successful.

Hoover Learning Outcomes

1. The student demonstrates habits of inquiry and knowledge in the following ways:

   • Demonstrates creativity by asking essential questions using habits of mind—evidence, connection, supposition, and significance
   • Distinguishes and states fact from opinion and/or acknowledges differing points of view
   • Demonstrates scientific inquiry by posing research questions, conducting research, and supporting decisions and solutions to problems with evidence

- Demonstrates mathematical logic, reasoning, and cause-and-effect relationships through problem solving
- Demonstrates the ability to apply decisions or solutions to future situations by making predictions, connections, and/or recommendations
- Demonstrates subject-matter knowledge through the use of inquiry and through evaluation or interpretations that are substantiated by examples or data from the discipline
- Uses appropriate electronic sources, including the Internet and CD-ROMs, to research, interpret, and process information

2. The student exhibits habits of work in the following ways:

- Plans and organizes time, money, people, or materials with written evidence of completing a project, event, or set of goals
- Demonstrates the ability to handle real-life issues in finance, time management, study habits, and day-to-day living
- Demonstrates the ability to collect, analyze, and organize resources and information
- Shows accountability to the group by following through on commitments, schedules, and responsibilities, and meets deadlines to achieve a shared goal or the needs of a client
- Documents different roles by establishing and operating self-directed work teams
- Evaluates self and peer performance in a group
- Demonstrates the use of computer platforms and a variety of software applications, including word processing, to compile, edit, polish, and preserve work
- Cites a variety of primary and secondary sources to validate research or to support a project
- Uses statistics to make generalizations from data
- Maintains a portfolio of selected work and achievements exhibiting the Hoover Learner Outcomes

3. The student communicates ideas and information in the following ways:

- Uses standard English in a variety of writing types and in verbal communication

- Uses the language of mathematics to communicate ideas and concepts and to explain reasoning and results
- Writes and speaks with clarity and with a sense of purpose
- Evaluates, corrects, and revises written, verbal, or other forms of communication
- Demonstrates listening, reading, and observational skills through written, verbal, and other types of responses
- Designs presentations and performances using organization, content, and visuals appropriate to the audience
- Selects appropriate graphics, charts, fonts, sounds, music, video, and other design elements for publications and presentations
- Teaches new skills and ideas to others while giving and receiving constructive feedback

4. The student plans for the future and shows a commitment to life-long learning in the following ways:

- Identifies and addresses career and personal priorities through the development of educational, career, and personal plans
- Seeks new information and understanding by exploring career opportunities through research, job shadows, and internships
- Demonstrates awareness and understanding of post–high school educational options and career choices
- Shows involvement and participation in fitness and recreation and demonstrates the importance of these activities as part of an ongoing fitness program
- Shows self-awareness of leisure choices and how these choices connect to lifelong plans
- Gives service to the school and outside community
- Uses technology that is relevant to the workplace and demonstrates understanding of common terms associated with technology
- Participates in voter registration

THE IMPACT OF STANDARDS-BASED REFORM

What is the impact of the standards-based reform initiative on students in urban schools? Intuitively, many people think that increasing educational standards ought to benefit all students. As it concerns students with diverse learning styles, parents and educators have long believed that raising expectations results in higher achievement. Educators often imagine that if our local school officials want to increase the percentage of students who score in the "proficient" or "mastery" categories on state assessments, they will want to increase all students' access to rigorous academic classes and effective teachers. We are encouraged by the thought that adopting higher expectations for students would lead to the dissolution of remedial classes such as Applied English, Functional Math, and Science Skills. Perhaps even greater numbers of students in urban schools might be enrolled in gifted and talented education (G.A.T.E.) and college preparatory classes, thus broadening their career options and their potential earning power as adults.

Furthermore, educators understand that adopting high standards for all students should promote the elimination of tracking and the inclusion of students with disabilities more fully in the mainstream of general education based on common learning standards for all students (Fisher, Sax, & Pumpian, 1999). In the context of standards-based reform, the curriculum is viewed as a unifying vehicle to ensure that a variety of students "master" the same information.

There is, unfortunately, another less positive scenario for describing the impact of standards-based reform on students who have traditionally been marginalized—students who qualify for Title 1 programs based on their family income, English-language learners, students with disabilities, and students in migrant education programs. What if states develop learning standards that do not reflect the needs of these students or others who traditionally have been only marginally included in the educational system? What if different standards are developed for different kinds of students—honors expectations for honors students, special education expectations for special education students, and so forth? If all students are not considered in the development of general standards or the design of curriculum frameworks, or if their test scores are not included in an aggregate district score, an even more segregated system of education might evolve. It is possible that schools would do more tracking, and some students would have less access to high-level curriculum than they do now. Fewer students might graduate with a high school diploma, and their future educational and career choices would continue to be limited.

RESPONSIVE CURRICULUM DESIGN

Determining what and how to teach all students—the content of the curriculum—requires that we examine more than just the body of knowledge that currently exists in particular academic disciplines. All students need to learn three types of skills:

- Content-area knowledge (in science, social studies, language arts, math, computers, the arts, etc.)
- Dispositions, social skills, and habits of mind (such as inquisitiveness, diligence, collaboration, work habits, tolerance, and critical thinking)
- Communication skills (such as reading, writing, speaking, and listening)

Educators concerned primarily with teaching students with diverse learning needs might wish that all schools would develop their curriculum—the content of what they teach—to address all three of these skill areas. If they did, it would be possible for any school to address any student's priority learning goals. No school would be "too academic," "too vocational," or "too devoted to the basics." And this could be accomplished by setting high standards for all.

Considering the variability in curriculum and instruction from district to district and school to school, we recommend that all teachers use some common curricular elements to design teaching/learning experiences that transcend philosophical differences and result in a learning environment that challenges and supports all students.

In addition to identifying the academic, communication, and social objectives for the unit, teachers need a way of communicating the overall focus of the unit to students. We suggest structuring a unit of study around an issue, topic, problem, or essential question. This creates a framework for the learning experience and provides direction and coherence (Friant, 2002; Jorgensen, 1994). In a standards-based curriculum, teachers generate these "central unit" issues with the standards firmly in mind. In a second-grade classroom, for example, the topic may be, How can I make connections while reading? Students can demonstrate their understanding of making connections with the text they read and current events. They can make connections between math concepts and real-world applications. Similarly, in an ancient civilization unit, for example, the issue might be, Are the Greeks still with us today? In this unit, students can demonstrate their mastery of several content standards, depending on the particular activities and products the teacher has planned. Students can illustrate that they understand the concepts of continuity and change in history, as well as principles and processes of social systems (such as the Olympics). They also should be able to comprehend and assess the content and artistic aspects of oral and visual presentations.

The question posed in a unit of instruction should not be one that can be answered with a simple yes or no or some other one-dimensional response. The question is not raised because the teacher already has a single "correct" answer in mind. Rather, the question should challenge each student to discover his or her own unique answer. The question, What is a hero? can serve to focus an interdisciplinary study on today's media portrayals of sports, political, and entertainment heroes, as well as examining why other heroes, such as those who contribute to their communities, are often overlooked. The use of an overarching central question can challenge students' ability to consider the complexities posed by many of the challenging issues in today's world.

Central unit issues, problems, topics, and questions serve as a way of focusing the teacher's planning as well. The use of this "backwards planning" approach (McTighe & Wiggins, 1999) allows the teacher to articulate to students exactly what the outcome of the unit will be. The culminating projects for the unit should include opportunities for students to respond to the question or problem first posed in the unit. Many teachers agree that backwards planning is one of the most effective approaches to project-based learning (Garry et al., 2003).

When all students in a classroom are focused on addressing a common question, differences in learning style and ability are less important than the commonality of all students constructing meaning in the content area, albeit in a personalized way. Well-crafted "essential questions" or problems offer challenge and accessibility to all students.

When the entire school is focused on essential questions at the same time, students can discuss their thinking about these questions during recess, school assemblies, passing periods, at lunch, and at other social times. This creates a schoolwide conversation about the overarching curriculum goals. Let's return to our second-grade example and the unit of study question, How can I make connections while reading? Each second-grade classroom in the school could create display boards for the school's Open House. Each classroom could design a way to show how students can make connections in all content areas. One classroom could display making connections among texts. Another classroom could display a board showing how students make connections with reading and art or reading and social studies. At Pojoaque Middle School, the essential question, What is a hero? was plastered around the school, placed on book covers in the library, read in the daily bulletin, and posted on the marquee for the community to see. We had evidence that the curriculum from this middle school became a community focus when we heard a waiter ask a group of students after school one day, "So what do you think about heroes now?"

STANDARDS IN THE CLASSROOM

Thus, the first step in responsive curriculum design is to identify the standards and expectations for the unit of study. Teachers identify specific content, social, and communication expectations for students from the state and local standards, the school's performance standards, and an understanding of the communication and social needs of children and young adults.

For example, in Mr. Giaquinto's kindergarten classroom, students are expected to know about Learning and Working Now and Long Ago. Mr. G wants his students to be familiar with career choices of the people in their surrounding community, as well as those of their grandparents and great-grandparents. These kindergarten students also need to discover how children's school lives have changed from that of long ago. Some of the goals Mr. G has for his students include being exposed to a variety of texts about jobs in the community, creating group murals together, and taking walking field trips around the school community.

In Ms. Pham-Barron's second-grade classroom, students are expected to learn about People Who Make a Difference. Ms. Pham-Barron wants her students to learn about the people in their school, community, city, and country. She expects students to read, write, research, and present information about people who have made a significant difference locally and beyond.

In Ms. Allen's fifth-grade classroom, students are expected to understand the economic forces that led to the need for world exploration. She also wants her students to understand the life of explorers, where explorers came from and where they went, and the variety of technological advances that made exploration of the "New World" possible.

In Ms. Mellander's seventh-grade math class, students are expected to understand how every rational number is either a terminating or repeating decimal. Students need to be able to convert terminating decimals into reduced fractions. The essential question which students are to answer during this unit of study is, How do we use rational numbers in our everyday lives?

Mr. Hernandez's ninth-grade English class focuses on the novel *Goodbye, Vietnam* (Whelan, 1993) as part of a grade-level focus on Knowing Yourself Through Others. The standards addressed in this unit include the student's ability to perform the following activities:

- Evaluate, interpret, summarize, and make connections through literature circles, shared reading, read-alouds, and journal responses
- Make predictions, infer information, and think beyond reading assignments
- Express thoughts and ideas using literature circles, journals, and visual representations
- Explore characters, setting, plot, climax, and themes in literature
- Gain a deeper understanding of characters through analysis of self
- Develop reading comprehension skills by using Post-it notes to mark important quotes/statements, identify literary symbols, construct open-ended questions, and decipher unknown vocabulary meanings
- Develop Internet search skills

Mr. Hernandez's essential question, which grew out of the grade-level standards and his students' prior knowledge, is, What are the sensory details that create imagery in the text?

In Ms. Grant's physics class, students are expected to solve problems involving elastic and inelastic collisions in one dimension by using the principles of conservation of momentum and energy. Specifically, Ms. Grant poses the following question to her students: When given the conditions for a collision, how can you use the law of conservation of momentum, along with energy equations, to solve for an unknown quantity?

Each of these teachers first considered the standards and expectations of the unit they wanted to plan. This first step allowed them to focus the unit, allocate instructional time for the unit of study, and plan instructional activities. Throughout this book, we return to these six classrooms as we outline the responsive curriculum design process. In addition to these six classrooms, the third section of this book contains a completed unit plan that may be useful in reviewing the curriculum design process.

Table 1.1 will be helpful as you see how lesson plans are developed. After each chapter you will see how the ideas begin to "grow" into effective lessons for your diverse learners and how responsive curriculum gets developed for all grade levels. (Note: All content standards are used as examples and are adopted by the California State Board of Education.)

WHAT DO YOU THINK?

1. What are some grade-level standards that you would like to use as a starting point for designing responsive curriculum? Jot these content and performance standards down.
2. Think about the standards and expectations at your grade level. What questions could you generate that are tied to these standards and appropriate for your students?
3. Thinking about backwards planning, what projects do you envision your students completing at the end of this unit of study?

Table 1.1. Standards/Expectations and Essential Questions

K	Grade 2	Grade 5	Grade 7	Grade 9	Grades 10–12
Standard: K.6 Students understand that history relates to events, people, and places of other times. **Question:** What are the differences between living today and living long ago?	**Standard: 2.5** Students understand the importance of individual action and character and explain how heroes from long ago and the recent past have made a difference in others' lives. **Question:** How have the actions of others impacted life in the past and today?	**Standard: 5.2** Students trace the routes of early explorers and describe the early explorations of the Americas. **Question:** What were were some of the entrepreneurial characteristics of early explorers and the technological developments that made sea exploration possible?	**Standard: 1.5** Students know that every rational number is either a terminating or repeating decimal and can convert terminating decimals into reduced fractions. **Question:** How do we use rational numbers in our everyday lives?	**Standard: 1.2** Students use precise language, verbs, and sensory details as they make predictions, infer, and gain a deeper understanding of characters through analysis of self. **Question:** What are the sensory details that create imagery in the text?	**Standard: 2G** Students know how to solve problems involving elastic and inelastic collisions in one dimension by using the principles of conservation of momentum and energy. **Question:** When given the conditions for a collision, how can you use the law of conservation of momentum, along with energy equations, to solve for an unknown quantity (such as velocity)?

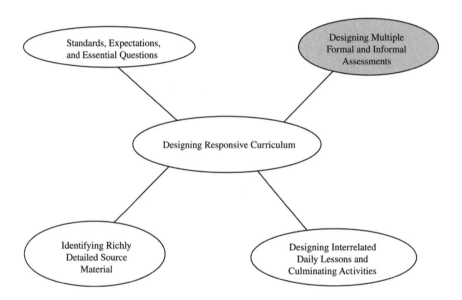

2

DESIGNING MULTIPLE FORMAL AND INFORMAL ASSESSMENTS

The keystone of effective assessment is the teacher's ability to articulate how students can demonstrate what they have mastered. What evidence will be accepted to show that each student has met the content and performance standards identified for the unit? Educators have long recognized that paper-and-pencil tests alone rarely provide students with the opportunity to show what they know, yet these assessments are sometimes done to the exclusion of richer performance-based assessments. And students with diverse learning styles may not always respond favorably to assessment methods that mine only verbal-linguistic and mathematical forms of intelligence.

Intelligence is comprised of many different kinds of abilities and talents (e.g., Gardner, 1999). While teachers historically emphasized verbal-linguistic and logical-mathematical intelligences to the exclusion of most other talents, teachers in responsive curriculum classrooms design instructional and assessment activities that tap into the multiple forms of intelligence possessed by all students. In this model, students have a range of ways to demonstrate what they know. For example, in a unit on inventions that utilizes all of the students' intelligences, musically inclined students study the science behind the invention of electronic music; "spatially smart" students build or draw a new invention; and students with strong linguistic and interpersonal intelligence form a discussion group and write "policy briefs" on the use of inventions that are intended to cause harm, such as the atomic bomb. These performance-based projects serve as a means of assessing the depth of knowledge a student has acquired while participating in the unit.

This provision of varied opportunities to demonstrate mastery carries a corresponding necessity to utilize multiple forms of assessment. To ensure powerful student learning, teachers monitor and assess students' progress throughout the unit, not just at the end. The greater diversity found in the classroom makes the need for periodic assessment critical. For these reasons, multiple assessments are important elements of responsive curriculum design. In order to strategically utilize assessments, an understanding of the types and purposes of assessments is required.

TYPES OF ASSESSMENTS

Formal Assessment

Assessments can be categorized into two broad fields: *formal assessments* and *informal assessments*. Tests that require a traditional, paper-and-pencil response to a series of questions with clearly "correct" answers are often considered to be formal assessments. Formal assessments share a fundamental construct: they measure student responses by comparing or referencing a particular exemplar. The exemplar they reference governs whether the test is *norm-referenced* or *criterion-referenced* (see Table 2.1). Norm-referenced tests measure a student's responses to a set of questions by comparing, or referencing, the scores of a group of similar students from other geographical locations (Flood, Lapp, & Wood, 1997). These instruments, also called standardized tests, are most commonly administered at regular intervals to large groups of students. For example, the CAT-6 is the norm-referenced test currently being used in California, whereas the California Standards Test (CST) is a standardized test based only on the content standards developed for the state of California. Criterion-referenced tests differ from norm-referenced tests because the exemplars in criterion-referenced tests are specific instructional objectives or standards. Large-scale criterion-referenced tests have been developed by some states to measure student progress on state standards (e.g., Florida Comprehensive Achievement Test, Michigan Educational Achievement Test). A more common application of criterion-referenced testing is the chapter test, given to students after the completion of instruction on a unit.

Both norm-referenced and criterion-referenced tests have limitations. Norm-referenced tests are most useful as a very broad measure of competency (Nezavdal, 2003; Stanley & Hopkins, 1972). A student's results on a standardized achievement test like the CAT-6 can document progress in content areas compared to other students around the country (Popham, 1999). However, such a test lacks the precision to diagnose a student's areas of weakness and strength within a content area (Chudowsky, 2003; Lapp & Flood, 1992).

Another limitation of norm-referenced tests is the restriction of the test items themselves. No single test could hope to query students on the entire body of knowledge contained in science, for example. Therefore, the test designers must limit the questions to a sampling of the content. Consequently, a student's performance on such a test is influenced by how closely the test design corresponds to that student's in-school and out-of-school science experiences.

Criterion-referenced tests also have shortcomings. The validity and reliability of a criterion-referenced test is dependent on how clearly the behavioral objectives are defined and how well the test item measures that behavioral objective. Straightforward facts like being able to identify geometric shapes in kindergarten are easy to assess. However, assessing whether or not a student can compare plane and solid objects by common attributes is difficult to assess. Similarly, students may be asked to name the five Great Lakes of the United States. This is simple and quick to assess. But assessing a student's understanding of the influence of these large bodies of water on the economic development of the region is more difficult to measure. A test maker is left with two equally unappealing choices: reduce the desired answer to the latter question to a simplified and easily measured response, or skip the item altogether in favor of the former question. Both choices challenge the test maker's ability to measure a student's higher order critical thinking skills.

Informal Assessment

In an era during which the broadly collected data from standardized tests is being used to make far-reaching educational decisions about large groups of students, it is vital that informal assessments also be recognized for their contribution to what is known about an individual student. Far more than standardized test results, which often do not arrive until the following school year, informal assessments are the tools educators rely on in daily instruction. *Informal assessments* are those selected and administered by the classroom teacher in order to determine what instruction needs to occur next. Astute classroom teachers possess a wealth of information about their students' knowledge of literacy and content and evaluate events such as book talks, classroom discussions, and permanent products to gauge students' progress and drive future instruction. Wise practitioners recognize the value of such informal assessments as a rich source of data.

Informal assessments differ from formal assessments because they do not require the systematic procedures for administering tests and interpreting test results (Leslie & Jett-Simpson, 1997). Many informal assessments are constructed by the teacher in an effort to measure a specific aspect of the curriculum. These informal assessments often consist of observations, skills checklists, portfolio assessments, conferencing, peer reviews, and self-assessments. Each category is discussed separately.

Table 2.1. Formal and Informal Assessments

Formal Assessment		
Type	Purpose	Procedure
Standardized Tests (Norm-Referenced)	To measure a student's performance in a variety of skills and compare those scores to students in other geographic locations	Administered at set intervals; students answer questions from booklet on standard forms
Criterion-Referenced Tests	To indicate attainment of mastery on specific instructional objectives, usually by answering a percentage of questions correctly	Administered with lesson plans; students read items and answer on separate paper

Table 2.1. *(continued)*

Formal Assessment		
Type	*Purpose*	*Procedure*
Teacher-made and Publisher-made Tests: True/False, Fill-in, Multiple Choice	To measure retention and comprehension of specific content	Administered within lesson plan; students answer focused questions in various formats

Informal Assessment		
Type	*Purpose*	*Procedure*
Observations	To assess a student's use of language in a variety of instructional settings	Observe and record student's use of language, often written in logs or journals
Skills Checklists	To track a student's development by noting which skills have become or are becoming part of a repertoire	Set up a checklist of desirable skills in language arts and periodically observe the student to determine which have been attained
Rubrics	To evaluate students by comparing their work to a preestablished set of criteria	Share rubric with students, collect student work and compare to rubric, share results with students with specific feedback
Portfolio Assessment	To document in a variety of ways how a student has developed as a language user	Teacher collects or student selects samples of work, including "published" writing, taped oral readings, conference notes
Conferencing	To provide opportunities for the teacher and student to discuss development	Student and teacher meet at set times to review performance and discuss instruction that may be required for student to progress
Peer Reviews	To involve students in the evaluation process and to build their evaluative and interactive skills	Give students guidelines for evaluation; two or more meet to discuss one another's work; peers' grade is factored into final grade
Self-Assessment	To empower students by making them responsible for and reflective of their own work	Students continually evaluate their performance and progress via checklists, interactions, inventories, conferences, and portfolios

Source: Adapted from Flood, Lapp, & Wood, 1997.

SEVEN ASSESSMENTS FOR RESPONSIVE CURRICULUM DEVELOPMENT

Observations

As students work in the classroom, teachers observe them and gain information about their knowledge and strategies. Sometimes these observations occur in unlikely settings, like on the playground or during an assembly. At other times, a teacher may deliberately construct a task in order to observe a student's response. Teachers frequently identify observations as the most important source of information about students (Copley, 2003; West, 1998). Yetta Goodman (1985) coined the term "kidwatching" to describe how astute teachers collect information about student performance. This is often accomplished through the use of anecdotal records—brief notes about a student's responses. Recording observations can be as simple as using a clipboard with Post-it notes in order to jot quick notes about a student's academic or social behavior. These notes are later added to a binder of pages, one for each student. Over time, the teacher can analyze these anecdotal records for patterns. Another way teachers can organize their observations of students is by using 5×7 index cards. The students' names can be written on the top of each card and the entire class of cards can be hooked together with a ring. As information begins to fill up, each card can be detached and added to a student's portfolio. (See Photo 2.1.)

Although teachers cannot possibly begin to document all their observations, documentation on some occasions can assist reflection and shar-

Photo 2.1.   Organizing Assessment Information With Index Cards and Portfolios

ing information with students, parents, administrators, and the next year's teacher. Telling a parent that his or her child has a difficult time contributing to book club discussions becomes more meaningful when the teacher's notes show that the child failed to participate in the group on three of the five observed occasions.

There are several guidelines for creating and maintaining anecdotal records to increase their usefulness. Many teachers favor using an anecdotal record form of their own creation. It is advisable to include the name of the student, the date, duration of the observation, and a description of the observed task data, which are beneficial when later analyzing the information gathered over several observations. See Form 2.1 for an example of an anecdotal record form.

Form 2.1.   Anecdotal Record Form

Name of Student: _____   Begin Time: _____

Date: _____   End Time: _____

Group Arrangement

Individual: _____   Partner: _____   Small Group: _____   Whole Class: _____

Description of Observed Task:

Observations:

A teacher might also construct an observational event in order to elicit student responses for the purpose of informing future instruction. An example of this is the KWL (what do we know/what do we want to know/what have we learned) chart (Ogle, 1986). When a first-grade teacher used a KWL at the beginning of a science unit on mammals, she discovered that her students were interested in finding out more about bats and how they differ from birds. Because this teacher believes in a constructivist approach to education (Bruner, 1966), she quickly found books to meet the needs of her curious students. The essential question for this unit of study became, Can birds and bats live together in a common habitat?

The KWL was revisited often throughout this unit as students began to add information to the L section (*what I learned*). As students received more information about bats and birds, their questions began to change and multiply. The W section (*what I want to know*) also began to get larger as a result of continuous inquiry. Similarly, when a sixth-grade teacher used this graphic organizer at the beginning of a social studies unit on ancient Egypt, he discovered that his students were interested in finding out about the lives of women and children in various social classes. He then applied this observational data by including the books *Growing Up in Ancient Egypt* (David, 1993) and *Women in Ancient Egypt: The Other Half of History* (MacDonald, 1999) into the readings his students would use to answer the central question, Would you survive in ancient Egypt? Observational assessment was also done at the end of this unit using the KWL chart. The last phase, *what I learned*, was done first in small groups and then completed in a classwide discussion. The teacher recognized that this instructional event served the multiple purposes of reinforcing new knowledge and providing him with a window on the progress of the class.

Skills Checklists

Checklists can also be helpful tools for documentation because they allow teachers to specify particular dimensions for observation and provide a means for summarizing those observations. Teachers may use a checklist to serve as a simple instrument for capturing students' evolving listening, reading, speaking, and writing skills. Many checklists are available in the literature on literacy practices (e.g., Allor, 2003; Clay, 1985; Harp, 1994; Ruddell, 1991; Sulzby, 1991). Checklists can also be designed to focus on a particular aspect of literacy instruction, such as a book club. The teacher can "listen in" to a book club discussion to note the strategies being used by readers in their effort to make meaning of the text. For example, an observation using a checklist of notable features of a book club discussion might reveal that two of the students are only rarely making connections between their comments and those of their peers. The teacher may then provide some specific instruction on using a graphic organizer to capture the group's ideas. An example of a checklist for use during a book club discussion can be seen in Form 2.2.

Form 2.2.   Book Club Checklist

Name of Student: _____   Date: _____
Discussion Text: _____

BOOK CLUB DISCUSSION BEHAVIORS	Not in Evidence	Emerging	In Use

Preparation:

Has read selection prior to group discussion

Has written in response journal

Has noted unfamiliar words or phrases

Group Behaviors:

Asks other group members questions about the text

Extends other students' responses

Respects the opinions of others

Connections:

Makes connections between text and self

Makes connections between focus text and other readings

Makes connections between text and other students' responses

Other Notes:

Rubrics

Rubrics are most often used in the assessment of writing, but are useful in other disciplines as well (Custer, 1995; Fitzgerald & Byers, 2002; Flood, Lapp, & Wood, 1997). For example, Leitze and Mau (1999) used a rubric to assess problem-solving activities in math. Huffman (1998) used a rubric to assess student learning in art production and notes that the rubric provided students with a visual guide as they completed their assignments. Finally, Carr (1997) used a rubric to assess his students' abilities to utilize current multimedia resources to combine sounds and images and produce a soundtrack for their lives.

By using rubrics, students are likely to understand the important elements for which they will be graded. Rubrics differentiate good from poor papers by providing students with criteria for each grade (Spandel & Stiggins, 1997). They also relieve the teacher of having to use subjective criteria for grading. While the development of the rubric is critical, teaching students how to use a rubric and understand the criteria of the rubric is even more important. Research suggests that when writing assessments only focus on mechanics, students' writing skills are not developed (Dahl & Farnan, 1998). Research also suggests that students should be involved in establishing the criteria for the rubric and, by doing so, more clearly understand the task at hand and can focus their performance toward the expected outcome. Table 2.2 provides an example of a writing rubric that may be useful for second grade and up. Photo 2.2 shows an example of a rubric constructed by the teacher and students in a kindergarten class. Keep in mind that teachers should use these as starting points and develop rubrics of their own in partnership with students.

Portfolio Assessments

Performance samples like portfolios refer to some form of student work that remains as an artifact for reflection by teachers, students, administrators, and parents. The original use of the term *portfolio* came from the collections of best works maintained by artists and architects. In education, portfolios more typically consist of samples that represent particular genres of tasks over a period of time rather than students' best work (Frey & Hiebert, 2003). Even so, the idea of examining samples of work that come from everyday settings, rather than from test settings, is

Table 2.2. Sample Writing Rubric

	Distinguished	Prominent	Proficient	Not Proficient
Thesis	Clearly defined, sustained throughout; topic effectively limited	Thesis defined; topic limited, but noted exceptions	Stated; attempt to limit topic	Unclear or unidentifiable; no attempt to limit topic
Development	Topic thoroughly developed throughout with specific examples to support thesis	Topic developed with reasonable evidence	Topic developed; general supporting evidence	Topic not clearly developed; unnecessary information
Organization	Highly organized plan with effective transitions; superior introduction and conclusion clearly relate to whole	Organized plan, but weak transitions; introduction or conclusion relate to the whole	Logical organization, with inconsistent transitions; introduction and conclusion do not clearly relate to whole	No organizational plan; no attempt to create unity; no transitions
Research	Ten or more qualified sources cited appropriately	Ten or more qualified sources but not cited appropriately	Fewer than 10 qualified sources cited	Fewer than 10 sources cited
Mechanics (e.g., punctuation, spelling, grammar)	Superior editing; fewer than five total errors in paper	Good editing; fewer than one error per page	Careful editing; fewer than two errors per page	Careless editing; more than two errors per page

Photo 2.2. Kindergarten Writing Rubric

restructuring assessment in many classrooms (Calfee & Gearhart, 1998). As with all assessment, portfolios require clearly defined goals and purposes, data collection that traverses time and task, and a system of interpretation (Calfee & Hiebert, 1991). A confusion of purpose can lead to the creation of portfolios that simply serve as collection bins of random student work (Wilcox, 1997). One way to establish clear purpose is to develop the expectations for the portfolio with students. In this manner, both student and teacher can brainstorm criteria for selection of pieces to go into the portfolio, as well as identify types of pieces that serve as evidence of mastery. This "portfolio pedagogy" (Yancey, 1992) can guarantee meaningful effort for both student and teacher.

Although the purposes of the portfolio shape its organizational structure, some elements are advisable for any portfolio. Winograd and Arrington (1999) suggest the following:

- A table of contents
- Samples of daily work
- Drafts and revisions of written work
- Student self-evaluations
- Goals written by the student, teacher, and family
- Student-teacher conference records
- Other observational information collected by the teacher

Portfolios are a powerful example of the recursive nature of assessment and instruction. When used well, they not only aid in the teaching of new skills but also support the continued polishing of students' habits of mind through guided reflection.

Conferencing

The act of conferencing with a student in a one-on-one setting can have a considerable effect on both participants, because the opportunities for such interactions are all too rare in busy classrooms. Conferences may be informal and relatively short (just a few minutes), or longer, with a structured script of questions to engage the learner. Either way, the goal of conferencing with a student is to promote the student's own ability to assess and reflect (Winograd & Arrington, 1999).

Much of the practice for this kind of classroom interaction comes from what we know about supporting student writers (Calkins, 1986; Glasswell, Parr, & McNaughton, 2003; Graves, 1983). In writing workshops, conferences are scheduled as the student's work evolves, creating multiple opportunities for the student to interact with the teacher (Dahl & Farnan, 1998). Teachers in responsive curriculum classrooms report that they need opportunities to talk in depth with individual students about specific topics or tasks, and the use of a structured conference form assists them in engaging in meaningful talk. An example of a conferencing form appears in Form 2.3.

Time is a teacher's most precious commodity, and finding opportunities to conference with students can be a challenge. Even so, setting time aside to talk with individuals can provide information teachers might not gain otherwise. While the task of meeting individually with 30 or 35 students may seem daunting, teachers in responsive curriculum classrooms set daily goals of conferencing with only one or two students. This can be achieved during sustained silent reading or during center rotations. By meeting daily with a small number of students, the teacher can conference with each member of the class over the course of a few weeks. Wise practitioners recognize that the investment of a bit of time to conference with a student promotes student self-reflection (Paris & Ayres, 1994). Photo 2.3 shows a teacher and a student conferencing about a piece of student work.

Photo 2.3. Teacher and Student Conferencing

Form 2.3.   Conferencing Form

Name of Student: _____   Date: _____
Description of student work used in this conference:

_____
_____
_____

Questions About Performance:
What do you like about this piece?

What would you change?

Questions About Process:
What was the best strategy you used to complete this piece?

What did you do when you had a problem with this piece?

Questions About Perception:
What makes you a good reader? A good writer?

What goals do you have for yourself this year?

Have you achieved the goals you have set for yourself?

What help do you need to reach your goals?

Peer Reviews

Teachers in responsive curriculum classrooms seek to move away from the outdated model of a teacher-centered classroom and toward student-centered learning and teaching. A promising practice in student-centered learning lies in the use of the peer reviews that are part of meaningful writing experiences (Atwell, 1998; Calkins, 1986). The goal of peer reviews is to involve students in the evaluation process and to build their evaluative and interactive skills (Flood, Lapp, & Wood, 1997). There are two commonly used forms of peer review. One is the peer conference, where a small group of students meets to discuss a work in progress. The other is in a large group setting, with a student sitting in the author's chair to share a piece (Cunningham, Hall, & Defee, 1998).

The "author's chair" provides an opportunity for a student to publicly read a finished work, while the peer conference provides a forum for a student writer to interact more intently with classmates while focusing on a composition in a formative stage. The reports of many teachers suggest that children become more knowledgeable about their command of writing and more motivated to continue to write as a result of such experiences (e.g., Freedman, 1995; Ganske, Monroe, & Strickland, 2003; Lobach, 1995). The success of peer involvement in writing suggests that such interactions hold promise for students' involvement in monitoring, planning, and assessing their comprehension. However, as with all classroom processes, the skills required to effectively collaborate with peers must be explicitly taught and monitored so that equity and communication difficulties can be circumvented (Henkin, 1995).

Self-Assessment

In many classrooms, the primary evaluator is the teacher. On those infrequent occasions when students participate in the assessment process, their involvement is nominal, such as checking a fellow student's work against the answers the teacher has written on the board. Far more rare is the classroom where children are asked to identify goals and monitor their progress toward those goals. The consequences of an exclusive reliance on externally driven assessment systems can have a negative effect on student achievement and attitude toward learning (Ames & Ames, 1984; Johnston & Winograd, 1985; Winograd & Paris, 1989). The use of self-assessment can serve as a motivator for students, as well as support their learning (Perry, 1998; Smith-D'Arezzo & Kennedy, 2004).

Several promising developments suggest greater student involvement in planning and monitoring learning. The emphasis of the last decade on brain-based learning is an example of such a development. Neurobiologists have shown that the search for meaning is innate, and that meaning emanates from the learner, not the teacher (Diamond & Hopson, 1998). Employment of self-assessment opportunities in daily practice increases each learner's ability to seek and identify goals that are personally meaningful.

Guides that assist students in self-assessment or in peer assessment are a feature in many literacy books and journals (e.g., Courtney & Abodeeb, 1999; Lapp, Fisher, Flood, & Cabello, 2000). Although such guides are popular in writing instruction, especially for editing and revising, some instruments are also oriented to aiding students in assessing their ability to plan and monitor their reading (e.g., Allen & Gonzalez, 1998). The self-evaluation guide in Form 2.4 is for self-assessment over the course of a culminating project. Students plan and reflect at the beginning, middle, and end of the project. This self-assessment then becomes part of the project itself. Students who are taught to plan and monitor their work habits begin to take ownership of their work.

Another example of guiding students in self-assessment comes from Project Zero (Chen, Krechevsky, Viens, & Isberg, 1998), which uses portfolios for assessment of writing and fine arts. While teachers interact with students in deciding what to put into portfolios, students are responsible for their selections. Furthermore, portfolios include a diary or journal in which students reflect on the progress they detect in their portfolio entries.

Assessing one's abilities and gauging the next step is an important part of any type of learning. This element has received increased attention in literacy programs, and indications are that emphases on metacognition and writing processes are creating more opportunities for students to assess their progress (Perchemlides & Coutant, 2004).

Form 2.4. Self-Assessment Form

Self-Assessment of Project Performance

Name: _____   Project: _____

Before Project: **Date:** _____
My goal(s) for this project:

Steps I need to take in order to meet my goal(s):

Mid-Project: **Date:** _____
Am I on target for meeting my goal(s)?

What do I need to do in order to meet my target?

Project Completion: **Date:** _____
Did I achieve my goal(s)?

Why or why not?

What are the strategies that worked for me?

What will I do differently next time?

ASSESSMENTS IN THE CLASSROOM

Let's return to our six teachers and essential questions to learn more about the ways in which assessments are used in their classrooms (see Table 2.3).

In order to assess what students know about living today and living long ago, Mr. Giaquinto uses a KWL chart to document what prior

Table 2.3. Standards/Expectations and Essential Questions and Assessments

	K	Grade 2	Grade 5	Grade 7	Grade 9	Grades 10–12
Standards/ Expectations and Essential Questions	**Standard: K.6** Students understand that history relates to events, people, and places of other times. **Question:** What are the differences between living today and living long ago?	**Standard: 2.5** Students understand the importance of individual action and character and explain how heroes from long ago and the recent past have made a difference in others' lives. **Question:** How have the actions of others impacted life in the past and today?	**Standard: 5.2** Students trace the routes of early explorers and describe the early explorations of the Americas. **Question:** What were some of the entrepreneurial characteristics of early explorers and the technological developments that made sea exploration possible?	**Standard: 1.5** Students know that every rational number is either a terminating or repeating decimal and can convert terminating decimals into reduced fractions. **Question:** How do we use rational numbers in our everyday lives?	**Standard: 1.2** Students use precise language, action verbs, sensory details, modifiers, active (not passive) voice. **Question:** What are the sensory details that create imagery in a poem?	**Standard: 2G** Students know how to solve problems involving elastic and inelastic collisions in one dimension by using the principles of conservation of momentum and energy. **Question:** When given the condition for a collision, how can you use the law of conservation of momentum, along with energy equations, to solve for an unknown quantity (such as velocity)?
Assessments	KWL, questioning, anecdotal notes, writing samples with accompanying rubrics	KWL, Venn diagram, questioning, anecdotal notes	KWL, quick write, oral reports, cloze passages, multiple choice test	Unit test, study guides, exit slips, vocabulary quizzes, checklist for daily schoolwork and homework	Journal entries, daily poems, homework, part of final exam	Construction of "egg safety device," written report describing device, momentum problems, momentum exam

knowledge students have about this topic and what they wish to learn. Throughout this unit, Mr. G uses questioning as a way to assess what students are comprehending about historical places and events and what material needs to be retaught. Mr. G uses writing samples with accompanying rubrics to find out what students are learning and how they are using writing conventions. Mr. G continuously takes anecdotal notes about his students' progress and keeps this important information in student portfolios.

Ms. Pham-Barron continuously assesses her students in order to inform her instruction. Like Mr. G, she uses graphic organizers, including KWL charts and Venn diagrams, to help her understand her students' prior knowledge and help to guide her instruction. Questioning her students and taking anecdotal notes help Ms. Pham-Barron document her students' progress and plan subsequent instruction based on her students' knowledge of heroes from long ago and the recent past.

Ms. Allen uses a variety of assessments with her fifth graders during her study of American explorers. For example, she uses an end-of-unit map test that she created to assess content knowledge, a writing rubric that the class developed to assess student writing, a peer evaluation worksheet to assess cooperative groups, a skills checklist and cloze passage to assess vocabulary development, and a KWL chart to assess information gained throughout the unit. Students are also evaluated on their oral presentations using an oral language rubric.

Like the other teachers, Ms. Mellander uses a variety of assessments before, during, and after instruction about rational numbers in her seventh-grade class. Ms. Mellander uses vocabulary quizzes, study guides and charts to assess work completed at centers and at home, and unit tests to assess her students' knowledge of terminating and repeating decimals. Additionally, Ms. Mellander asks her students to do a quick write at the end of lessons as an "exit slip" out of class.

Mr. Hernandez uses a number of assessments while his ninth-grade students answer the essential question: What are the sensory details that create imagery in the text? During the literature circles, he uses a Book Club checklist in which students assess themselves while working collaboratively in a group. He also uses a checklist to assess his students' ability to conduct Internet searches. He uses a KWL chart to understand his students' knowledge of Vietnam and immigration. Further, he uses a writing rubric to assess students' character analysis papers and their literature circle journal entries. Finally, he requires that students regularly self-assess their performance and behavior in his classroom.

Ms. Grant expects her high school students to be able to use the law of conservation of momentum to solve for an unknown quantity. In order to assess this, Ms. Grant uses rubrics for written reports describing the students' "egg safety" device, the construction of the egg-safety device, short answers to momentum problems, and a momentum exam.

Ongoing assessment is also an important way to monitor student progress. These formative assessments allow the teacher to determine if all students are assuming more control of the content as instruction progresses. A student who is not making sufficient progress can be retaught using a classroom peer tutor, or in a teacher-directed small group with others who could benefit from a review of the material. As our table begins to grow, you can see how assessment information is used to assess students' knowledge of the essential questions and content standards.

WHAT DO YOU THINK?

1. How is assessment related to instruction?
2. What types of assessments have you used in your classroom? What do these assessments tell you?
3. Which assessments do you find most useful? Which are least useful? Why?
4. Jot down a few types of assessments you will try out in the next couple of weeks. Be sure to reflect on how they worked for you.

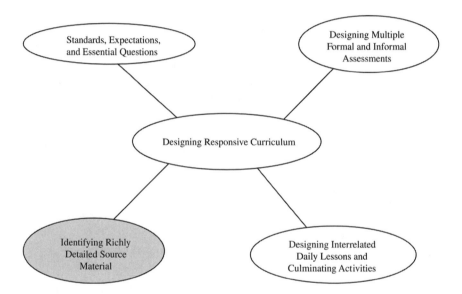

Standards, Expectations, and Essential Questions

Designing Multiple Formal and Informal Assessments

Designing Responsive Curriculum

Identifying Richly Detailed Source Material

Designing Interrelated Daily Lessons and Culminating Activities

❸

IDENTIFYING RICHLY DETAILED
SOURCE MATERIAL

The use of richly detailed source material that represents a variety of student learning styles and intelligences ensures that each student in the class has access to the knowledge base in the topic being studied (Manner, 2001; Onosko & Jorgensen, 1997). Too often, teachers put students with reading difficulties at a distinct disadvantage from the start by failing to augment print-based information sources. Textbooks used in content instruction can be limiting when they are used to the exclusion of other materials. For example, most students would better understand a lecture on DNA if the teacher included an activity wherein the students take apart and put together a three-dimensional model of the complex double-helix molecule. Similarly, in a first-grade classroom, students would understand the concept of sinking and floating by engaging in hands-on learning in which objects are placed in a tub of water. Thus, this chapter provides a discussion about selecting materials that are appropriate and responsive to the needs of students and how to use the textbook and other richly detailed sources.

USING TEXTBOOKS EFFECTIVELY

Using content standards requires teachers to continue to emphasize the textbook as a primary source (Massich & Munoz, 1996) while developing lessons in which students can experience learning through hands-on activities (Christ, 1995). Relying on the text is not unfamiliar to teachers (Squire, 1987). However, doing so and also meeting all of these additional challenges is often overwhelming. During social studies instruction, teachers usually rely even more heavily on books to create images of the past (Moss, 1991) and to explore the majority of social studies issues. In fact, several studies have shown that, in elementary schools, the textbook composes as much as 90% of the instructional time in social studies (Shaver, Davis, & Helburn, 1980; Woodward, Elliott, & Nagel, 1986).

But the textbook cannot do the whole job alone. Many other sources are needed to supplement the textbook. The types of books and materials selected by teachers for social studies units have received increased attention over the past decade (Lapp, Flood, & Farnan, 1996; Ross, 1997). Consider the perspective offered by a textbook: It serves as a summary of the textbook authors' knowledge of the content. While valuable, it is several degrees removed from the primary-source information used by the authors in developing the textbook. When all the events and historical figures of World War II may occupy a few pages in the world history textbook, there is little room for the details. Since textbooks can only rarely provide a comprehensive picture of the period of study, instruction often becomes focused on memorizing the facts and chronology of events. History textbooks, while presenting correct factual information (Romanowski, 1996), often provide a narrow, singular perspective (Banks, 1973; Tunnell & Ammon, 1996).

With widespread attention being given to the integration of literacy across the curriculum during the past 10 years, many teachers who use the textbook as a resource also supplement it with literature selections (Combs & Beach, 1994; Daniels & Zemelman, 2003; Johnson & Ebert, 1992; Moss, 1991). The difficulty of the textbooks is also problematic for many readers. The textbooks themselves are written at an assigned grade level, and the readability of the text excludes many students from access to the material held in its chapters. The gold standard for reading is the ability to comprehend—to make meaning of the words on the page. But when text is at a frustration level for some students (typically defined as reading 89% or less of the words correctly), comprehension is compromised. Without other supporting materials, these students slip further behind their classmates in content knowledge.

The range of student reading levels in all classrooms requires teachers to plan curriculum in a different fashion. Wise practitioners plan for a span of four grade levels (two below grade level, at grade level, and one above grade level) in order to increase access to the content. This is not as difficult as it may appear, because teachers using responsive curriculum design recognize that the textbook is merely one source, and not the definer of the curriculum itself. Using a unit organized around a central question, a teacher can then assemble a wide range of materials in many mediums and at many readability levels. In a third-grade class, students are much more likely to understand the likelihood of future volcano eruptions after watching a National Geographic video on Mt. St. Helens, reading *Magic School Bus Blows Its Top* (Cole, 1996), and building and erupting their own volcanoes in the classroom. In a tenth-grade world history class, the teacher knew the students would better understand a lecture on World War II and the Holocaust if the source materials included the textbook, a videotape of a survivor, actual letters written during the time in *Anne Frank: The Diary of a Young Girl* (Frank & Mooyaart, 1993), and personal interviews with their family members who lived during the war. Through the use of multiple mediums, the teacher created source materials at differing reading levels without compromising the integrity of the information. This teacher recognized that the teaching of history is the teaching of stories, and that the complexities of people's lives are best represented in the histories of individuals. The use of these richly detailed source materials also better equips the students to answer the central question, How does war affect those who do not fight?

INTERMEDIALITY

The world has been profoundly affected by the explosion of available information. For instance, technology has shortened the production time necessary to write books. Twenty years ago, there were approximately 5,000 children's books in print; in 1999, that figure had reached 89,000. Delivery of information has also rapidly expanded into mediums that did not yet exist even a decade ago. The Internet has become a major force in the dissemination of information, few businesses today are without a website, and customers increasingly expect the Internet to be the point of sale.

The expansion of information sources creates new demands on to-day's learner. Viewing is now recognized as a dimension of literacy, along with speaking, listening, reading, and writing (Flood & Lapp, 1995). In-creased reliance on media and technology has led to new understand-ings of literacy and learning (Lapp, Flood, & Fisher, 1999; Semali & Pailliotet, 1999). Flood and Lapp (1995) propose a "broader conceptu-alization in which literacy is defined as the ability to function compe-tently in the 'communicative arts,' which include the language arts as well as the visual arts of drama, art, film, video, and television" (p. 1).

These new forms of visual and information literacy are changing the very nature of schooling (Dahl & Farnan, 1998; Messaris, 1994). For ex-ample, one new area of inquiry focuses on accessing information through multiple forms of media—intermediality. While a consensus definition of intermediality has yet to emerge, generally speaking, it in-volves multiple forms of both text and media, including books, videos, life experiences, websites, films, posters, CD-ROMs, illustrations, and the like. Advances in technology significantly influence these multiple forms of media. Technology permeates our world—cellular phones, computers, fax machines, and VCRs, just to name a few. Students in our schools must not only learn to read, they must also learn to access in-formation for a variety of purposes.

Recent research indicates that using multiple sources of information in-creases comprehension, critical thinking, and recall (Lapp, Flood, & Fisher, 1999; Koretz, 1999). Frey (1998) reports increased levels of un-derstanding and more frequent responses at the aesthetic level when her fourth graders had access to multiple information sources. Similarly, Mas-sich and Munoz (1996) describe the success they experienced with their middle school students, especially English-language learners, as they taught a Civil War unit with multiple information sources, including visu-als, realia, music, documents, and diaries. Evans (1997) suggests that social studies instruction should be based on inquiry, problem solving, and critical thinking. It seems that if this type of instruction were to become a reality, the use of multiple and varied sources would motivate students to become active thinkers who are challenged by alternative viewpoints.

TYPES OF SOURCE MATERIALS

Children's and Young Adult Literature

Historical and realistic fiction written for young readers serves as a boon for teachers in responsive curriculum classrooms. The use of trade books not only infuses well-written literature into the curriculum, it also provides multiple perspectives at varied levels of text difficulty. The availability of literature for use in content areas has expanded rapidly in the last decade. By example, when studying diverse and different communities in social studies, a teacher may stock her bookshelves with easy readers, such as *Angel Child, Dragon Child*, by Michele Maria Surat (1989), or more challenging chapter books, like *Pioneers*, by John Artman (1987).

Likewise, in addressing the range of reading levels in a history classroom studying the role of children in the Middle Ages, a teacher offers several different pieces of literature. Using the criteria of well-written fiction featuring a child protagonist in a medieval setting, students can read either *Catherine, Called Birdy* (Cushman, 1995), *Adam of the Road* (Vining, 1987), or *Otto of the Silver Hand* (Pyle, 1967). While the three books reflect a wide range of readability, all are united in setting and theme. The large-group discussions facilitated by the teacher lead to the creation of a graphic organizer synthesizing each book's main characters, the problems they face, and the solutions to those challenges. These student responses are then compared to the information presented in the textbook, assisting students in connecting the protagonists' stories to historical events.

Poetry

The power of poetry as a richly detailed source material lies in its economy of words. Well-chosen poetry selections can convey content knowledge, as well as carry an emotional message. The accessibility of poetry can encourage reluctant readers. For instance, science text on insects can be augmented with the fourteen bug poems of *Joyful Noise: Poems for Two Voices* (Fleischman, 1988). Paralleling a study of the migration of workers from Mexico, the experiences of Mexican American children in the southwestern United States are represented in *Canto Familiar* (Soto, 1996). Weather and seasons are beautifully portrayed in the Japanese haiku poetry of Issa and Basho, in such collections as *Cool Melons-Turn to Frogs! The Life and Poems of Issa* (Gollub, 1998) and *Grass Sandals: The Travels of Basho* (Spivak, 1997). Even complex geometry and algebra concepts can be portrayed through the use of the poems in *Math Talk: Mathematical Ideas in Poems for Two Voices* (Pappas, 1991). Other collections by notable poets contain myriad subject matter. These include the works of Jack Prelutsky (1996) in *Pizza the Size of the Sun* and Carl Sandburg (1995) in *Poetry for Young People*.

Biographies and Autobiographies

Biographies of historical figures offer the richness of human experience, set in the context of notable events in history. Many biographies of children and adults facing extraordinary circumstances exist in popular literature. Biographies can also be used to explore an entire genre of experience. A study of notable book authors gives students an opportunity to connect popular works with a writer's experiences. A unit of instruction could examine the lives of Jerry Spinelli (1998) in *Knots in My Yo-Yo String: The Autobiography of a Kid* and Gary Paulsen (1999) in *My Life in Dog Years*. The experiences of Japanese citizens and Japanese American citizens during World War II are examined in the books *Shin's Tricycle* (Kodama, 1995), *Sadako and the Thousand Paper Cranes* (Coerr, 1999), and *The Invisible Thread: An Autobiography* (Uchida, 1995). And, of course, biographies can also be used to focus on a remarkable life. Examples include *Girl of the Shining Mountains: Sacagawea's Story* (Roop, 1999), *The Amazing Life of Benjamin Franklin* (Giblin, 2000), *Escape from Slavery: The Boyhood of Frederick Douglass in His Own Words* (Douglass, 1994), *Meet the Great Composers* (Montgomery & Hinson, 1995), *Lives of the Musicians: Good Times, Bad Times (and*

What the Neighbors Thought) (Krull, 1993), and *Sebastian: A Book About Bach* (Winter, 1999). Biographies present a fascinating window on the lives of the famous, the infamous, and those thrust into extraordinary circumstances.

Picture Books

Picture books? Yes, picture books can provide older students an interesting look at a topic of study (Goerss, 1998). Picture books also reinforce vocabulary, language skills such as word rhyming, and story sequence. Picture books have been successfully used in middle school classrooms to encourage reluctant readers to participate in content-area instruction (Cassady, 1998). Miller (1998) believes that picture books build connections to learning experiences for early adolescents in all content areas. Picture books have been used as a supplement to the textbook in many upper grade and secondary school classrooms across the country. For example, Beck, Gilles, O'Connor, and Koblitz (1999), provide a list of 33 books, including picture books, that give children insight into living in the Midwest and into westward expansion. Mundy and Hadaway (1999) used picture books about weather to provide supplemental instruction for high school ESL students. Matanzo and Richardson (1998) describe how the picture book rendition of the operatic story *Aida* was used with secondary school students to introduce operas. Awards such as the Newbery and the Caldecott Medals are given yearly and also provide educators with information about new books. The Newbery Award is based on literary quality, the Caldecott on the quality of the illustrations. The medal and honor winners are selected by committees that read all of the books published during the year.

The Coretta Scott King Award is presented annually to both an African American author and an African American illustrator for outstanding contributions to children's literature. Organizations such as the International Reading Association (IRA) and the National Council of Teachers of English (NCTE) have established committees that annually develop lists of notable books. IRA's Teacher's Choices is a national project involving teachers in the selection of books for use across the curriculum. The Teacher's Choices lists are published annually in *The Reading Teacher*.

Diaries and Letters

Students often view the lives and events of the past as disconnected and irrelevant to their lives. History through this lens becomes simply a task of memorizing dates and names for later use on a test. The use of ephemera (papers that reflect a historical era or event) in classrooms can breathe life into historical topics. While actual items are not available outside museums, many letters, journals, and diaries have been reproduced for student use. Probably the most famous is the Anne Frank diary, and others are available as well. An outstanding example is *We Are Witnesses: Five Diaries of Teenagers Who Died in the Holocaust* (Boas, 1996). Besides telling the story of Anne Frank, four other teens relate their experiences, serving as a chilling reminder of just how many lives were taken in the Holocaust. *Zlata's Diary: A Child's Life in Sarajevo* (Filipovic, 1995) is the journal of an eleven-year-old child in war-torn Bosnia.

A teacher can first present the factual information about an important event, then contrast it with an entry from a diary. *Anastasia's Album* (Tanaka, 1996) is designed like a scrapbook, and tells the story of Anastasia, youngest daughter of the last czar of Russia. Photographs, drawings, letters, and other memorabilia reflect Anastasia's life up until her death at the hands of revolutionaries at the age of eleven. Younger students can learn about the life of Benjamin Banneker, a noted African American astronomer and almanac author, in *Dear Benjamin Banneker* (Pinkney, 1998). Excerpts of letters between Banneker and Thomas Jefferson are used to tell the story of these two remarkable Americans. The diaries and letters used in class can be extended by having students write original journal entries about the lives they are studying. This use of simulation in writing can increase a student's understanding of the concepts being taught (Schneider & Jackson, 2000).

Music

Music is a powerful way to motivate students to read (Towell, 1999–2000). Not only do students read the song texts, but they often become interested in a topic of study and search out books related to the songs they like. For example, Alvermann and Hagood (2000) found that focusing on students' music interests led to increased interest in school literacy practices. The challenge for teachers is to find appropriate music for the content they teach. Probably the easiest way to do this is to collaborate with the music educator at the school site. In addition, several websites related to children's music exist (http://www.childrensmusic .org/). Some examples of the use of music in content-area instruction include the song "Follow the Drinking Gourd" as the introduction to a unit of study on slavery. A ninth-grade English teacher used the song "Isn't It Ironic" to focus on irony in novels. A tenth-grade earth science teacher collected a number of songs, including "Oh, Watch the Stars," "Haley Came to Jackson," and "Star Light, Star Bright" to remind students about the cultural interest in the night sky.

Websites

The emergence of the Internet as a source for material to use in classrooms has challenged many teachers. After all, most teachers' experience in school did not include Internet resources. Additionally, there are many warnings about students accessing inappropriate websites that feature violence, pornography, and hate speech. The combination of being unsure of how to use Internet resources in the classroom and concern about the content of websites has made some educators reluctant to use these source materials. However, students need to be competent at locating Web sources and analyzing the worthiness of the content. Judicious use of Internet resources can teach students both of these important skills.

The first step in using websites as source material is determining whether they serve a purpose. Internet sources should not be used simply to fulfill a technology requirement, but rather should be utilized when they offer information that expands students' understanding of the concepts being taught. When exploring potential Internet websites for use in the classroom, ask these questions:

1. Does this site contain information that is accurate?
2. Would the site be easy to use by students?
3. Does it identify the hosting institution?
4. When was it last updated?
5. Are there links to other sites? Are those links of similar quality?

When suitable websites have been identified, the next step is to con-struct opportunities for students to use them. Many teachers introduce websites to their students by creating a learning station for use in center rotations. The teacher bookmarks the websites in advance, then creates a task for students to complete. A simple introductory lesson for a new web-site is a scavenger hunt. An excellent site is www.nationalgeographic.com/kids. A scavenger hunt for this site could target regular features of the site, including its geography bee, pen pals network, and amazing facts. This al-lows students to practice scrolling and navigating around the site while cre-ating a challenge for them to complete. As students become more com-fortable with the mechanics of a website, more can be introduced, this time with the task being to use the content the site offers.

In a unit about planets, a teacher bookmarked the National Geo-graphic site; www.discovery.com, sponsored by the Discovery Channel; and http://kids.msfc.nasa.gov, the NASA website designed for students. Students used these three websites for information about their group's planet, along with more conventional sources. Other outstanding web-sites that serve as excellent reference materials include www.louvre.fr, which provides an online tour of the Louvre's collection, and www.whitehouse.gov/WH/kids/html/home.html, for information about the president and the U.S. government.

The ultimate goal for students is to be able to evaluate websites them-selves, so that they can critically analyze information. Like other forms of information, Internet websites represent wide variability in terms of quality, accuracy, and design. This means that students require explicit instruction on how to view Internet information, and need to be taught to ask questions, much like those a teacher asks when examining a po-tential website. This may be done in the form of a rubric. An example of a rubric for student use appears in Form 3.1.

Guest Speakers

Collaboration between schools and community members is not a new idea. However, at the secondary level, many school personnel do not know how to effectively use community members as part of the cur-riculum. Guest speakers are one way that professionals or community members with unique experiences or lives can be invited into the school system (Wortmann, 1992). Guest speakers allow students to talk with a

Form 3.1. Student Rubric for Evaluating Internet Websites

Website Address: _____

Name of Hosting Institution: _____

	Outstanding	Adequate	No Evidence
Ease of Use:			
Easy to load			
Clear site map available			
Help available			
Design:			
Links to other sites work			
Good use of graphics			
Text fits on one page			
Content:			
Accuracy of information			
Completeness of information			
Linked sites are of similar quality			
Credibility:			
Contact information available			
Host institution named			
Site is regularly updated			

variety of people about historical events, career options, new developments in technology, life experiences, and so on (Pokrywcaynski, 1992; Tunseth & Nowicki, 2003).

Finding good guest speakers can be a trial-and-error process. Potential guest speakers must be invited, listened to, and evaluated by the teachers and students. At least three important considerations for guest speakers must be considered. First, the speaker's style is important. Does this person have the presentation skills necessary to engage young adults? Second, the speaker's qualifications are important. Does this person have the background to answer questions that students will have? Finally, the content of the speech is important. Does this person understand the age-appropriate nature of the content? Does this person understand the curriculum of the class and how his or her speech will support the overall curriculum? Sometimes guest speakers need to be reminded to bring audiovisual materials with them—especially if they have artifacts from the field or historical events.

To ensure that students attend to the guest speaker, teachers often require students to take notes during the presentation and to submit those notes for review by the teacher. In addition, many teachers spend the class session prior to the arrival of the guest speaker identifying questions in advance so that the audience can participate in a meaningful conversation with the guest speaker. Teachers have found that identifying questions in advance also provides some anticipation and interest in the guest speaker's presentation. Students also benefit from the availability of a graphic organizer to capture their observations. An example of such an organizer is shown in Form 3.2.

Using the Community as a Classroom

Instruction outside of classroom walls provides teachers and students with opportunities to apply what has been learned within a real-world context. It reinforces the importance and usefulness of what has been learned previously, while challenging students about new areas to explore. We hesitate to use the words *field trip*, because that terminology represents an outdated model of the trip itself as a culminating activity. Rather, we prefer to view the world as a classroom, with trips as an extension of teaching and learning.

In order to maximize the impact of a community visit, students must be prepared for the experience. Community experiences are an ideal opportunity to expand the vocabulary of students, particularly English-language learners. However, their initial exposure to the new vocabulary should not be in the community. Vocabulary instruction must first occur

---

Form 3.2.   Student Evaluation for Guest Speaker

Speaker: _____

Topic: _____

1. I thought the things the speaker said were interesting.

        Yes   No   Somewhat

2. I understood what the speaker was discussing.

        Yes   No   Somewhat

3. I would like to learn more about this topic or profession.

        Yes   No   Somewhat

4. I know more about this topic or profession than I did before this guest speaker.

        Yes   No   Somewhat

5. This profession interests me as a possible career choice.

        Yes   No   Somewhat   Not Applicable

6. The three most important things that I learned during this presentation are:

7. The questions that I still have include:

---

in the classroom, so that learners can then refine their understanding through the community experience.

USING INFORMATION SOURCES IN CLASSROOMS

Information sources permeate the classrooms of our focus teachers. Each has a well-stocked classroom library with over 400 titles in each classroom, which is often used for independent reading. Thus, in addition to the school library, students in these classrooms can access poetry, children's literature, biographies, and picture books at any time. Beyond the classrooms libraries, these six teachers incorporate additional information sources based on their unit of study. Let's return to our teachers to see how their units of study are growing.

Mr. G wants his kindergartners to not only listen to books about living today and long ago but also to "see" the differences. He brings in videos, photos, and pieces of clothing so his second-language students can touch the realia and discuss the similarities between historical and present-day artifacts.

Ms. Pham-Barron also wants her second-grade students to see geographical locations in which heroic Americans made history. Maps and timelines fills this second-grade classroom in addition to photos, pictures books, and the social studies text. Students gain additional insight about these Americans by listening to famous speeches and watching videos about historical events.

In Ms. Allen's unit on explorers, she invites students to use a computer program about explorers, the social studies text, maps of the world, and a compass. She reads aloud several books to her class, including *Explorers* (Fradin, 1984), *Six Brave Explorers: A Pop-Up Book* (Moerbeek & Dijs, 1997), and *Follow the Dream* (Sis, 1996). The students also visit the local space exploration museum during one class day in order to receive hands-on learning about different explorers.

In Ms. Mellander's seventh-grade math class, students study their textbook, take notes, complete decimal equivalent activity sheets, and play a math Bingo game. Ms. Mellander brings in accountants, financial planners, and math professors so students can interact with mathematicians in everyday life.

Mr. Hernandez uses the novel *Goodbye, Vietnam* (Whelan, 1993) as the core book for his ninth-grade unit. He begins his unit of study with a read-aloud of the picture book *Who Belongs Here? An American Story* (Knight, 1993). In addition, he invites students to view websites about Vietnam, view a video about a dramatic rescue of a refugee boat in Indonesian waters, keep diaries as if they were forced to leave their homes, read the diaries and other personal narratives from the book *Voices from Vietnam* (Denenberg, 1997), learn at least one poem from the book *An Anthology of Vietnamese Poems: From the Eleventh*

Through the Twentieth Centuries (Huynh, 1996), and discuss immigration experiences with an adult who was a recent arrival from Vietnam. He also adds a number of children's picture books about Vietnam to his classroom library, including *Journey Home* (McKay, 1998), *The Lotus Seed* (Garland, 1997), and *The Crystal Heart: A Vietnamese Legend* (Shepard, 1998).

Ms. Grant uses many picture and experiment books with her physics students, including *Gizmos and Gadgets: Creating Science Contraptions That Work* (Hauser, 1999) and *Janice VanCleave's Physics for Every Kid: 101 Easy Experiments in Motion, Heat, Light, Machines, and Sound* (VanCleave, 1991). High school students uses their physics textbook, supplemental handouts on momentum, and Cornell notes forms, and watch videos about the topic, including *Momentum* (Ianzelo & Low, 2002) and *Standard Deviants School Physics Companion* (Cerebellum Corp., 2002). See Table 3.1 for more information.

WHAT DO YOU THINK?

1. Think about the range of reading abilities in your classroom. At what grade levels are your students reading? What materials will you be sure to use to meet all your students needs?
2. Who could you invite into your classroom to speak to students about your unit of study? Think about school-based experts and those in the community. Where might you take your students to expand their knowledge of your topic?
3. Thinking about learning styles and intelligences, what materials would work best with your bodily-kinesthetic learners? Spatial learners? Musical learners? Others?

Table 3.1. Standards/Expectations and Essential Questions, Assessments, and Materials

	K	Grade 2	Grade 5	Grade 7	Grade 9	Grades 10–12
Standards/ Expectations and Essential Questions	**Standard: K.6** Students understand that history relates to events, people, and places of other times. **Question:** What are the differences between living today and living long ago?	**Standard: 2.5** Students understand the importance of individual action and character and explain how heroes from long ago and the recent past have made a difference in others' lives. **Question:** How have the actions of others impacted life in the past and today?	**Standard: 5.2** Students trace the routes of early explorers and describe the early explorations of the Americas. **Question:** What were some of the entrepreneurial characteristics of early explorers and the technological developments that made sea exploration possible?	**Standard: 1.5** Students know that every rational number is either a terminating or repeating decimal and can convert terminating decimals into reduced fractions. **Question:** How do we use rational numbers in our everyday lives?	**Standard: 1.2** Students use precise language, verbs, and sensory details as they make predictions, infer, and gain a deeper understanding of characters through analysis of self. **Question:** What are the sensory details that create imagery in the text?	**Standard: 2G** Students know how to solve problems involving elastic and inelastic collisions in one dimension by using the principles of conservation of momentum and energy. **Question:** When given the condition for a collision, how can you use the law of conservation of momentum, along with energy equations, to solve for an unknown quantity (such as velocity)?

Assessments	KWL, questioning, anecdotal notes, writing samples with accompanying rubrics	KWL, Venn diagram, questioning, anecdotal notes	KWL, quick writes, oral reports, cloze passages, multiple choice test	Book Club checklists, Internet checklists, KWL, writing rubrics, self assessments	Journal entries, homework, Book Club checklist, KWL, self assessments	Construction of "egg safety device," written report describing device, momentum problems, momentum exam
Materials	Picture books, videos, photos, realia of clothing, pots and pans, tools, pictures of one-room schoolhouses	Maps, timelines, picture books, famous speeches, videos, social studies textbook	Computer programs, social studies text, maps of the world, compass, picture books, field trip to museum	Math textbook, teacher generated notes, Decimal Equivalents activity sheet, Bingo game, math experts	Core book, picture books, websites, diaries and personal narratives, poetry, guest speakers	Cornell notes form, Physics textbook, supplemental handouts on momentum, videos, picture books

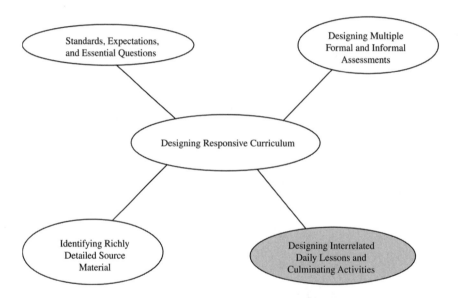

4

DESIGNING INTERRELATED DAILY LESSONS AND CULMINATING ACTIVITIES

All students need to have explicit connections made among individual daily learning experiences. Teachers must ensure that daily activities logically build students' knowledge throughout the unit to enable them to use the newly acquired body of knowledge to answer the overarching unit question. For example, the following set of three activities might accomplish this goal: identifying various viewpoints or positions regarding the unit's central issue or problem; identifying key concepts, events, or persons related to the issue under consideration; and identifying and answering questions that need to be considered to intelligently address the problem or issue.

For example, while reading *Of Mice and Men* (Steinbeck, 1937), students create character webs and concept maps based on the book. Character webs are updated after each chapter—students illustrate characters as they meet them and write phrases that describe the individual (with page number references) around the illustration. Similarly, students can use character webs in primary grades while listening to *Charlotte's Web* (White, 1974) read aloud. Students can draw pictures and phrases about how the characters have changed as the plot thickens. Concept or semantic maps are spatial representations of the main points of the chapter completed in groups of four students (for more information, see Lapp, Flood, & Hoffman, 1996). Reviewing the character webs and concept maps allows the teachers to assess their students' comprehension. Additional assessments, such as quick writes, found poems, and impromptu speeches, allow teachers to gauge the learning of everyone in the class. Thus, this chapter focuses on instructional design and culminating projects.

INSTRUCTIONAL DESIGN

Stephen Covey, an organizational management and leadership mentor, advises to begin with the end in mind (Covey, 1990). His words are just as true when discussing lesson planning. Experienced teachers know the value of planning to ensure that learning occurs for all students. And key to effective planning is the ability to articulate what the student outcomes will be and how they will be evidenced. Questions to ask when planning a lesson include the following:

- What are the key concepts?
- What should students do with these concepts?
- What activities will provide students with the opportunity to practice these concepts?
- How much time is available?
- What assessment methods will be used to determine students' mastery?

Teachers in responsive curriculum classrooms also acknowledge the social nature of teaching and learning (Green, Harker, & Golden, 1987). The most carefully crafted lesson can fail dismally if the teacher does not recognize the reciprocal relationship between instructor and learners in revising and reshaping the lesson in progress. As students gain (or fail to gain) understanding of the lesson, the demands of the lesson may shift, necessitating the reteaching or extension of the original concepts. In effective lessons, careful planning is coupled with attention to the interactions of students to continually reconstruct the lesson (Doyle, 1996). Many models of lesson plan frames exist (e.g., Hunter, 1994; Macdonald & Purpel, 1987; Slavin, 1995), but nearly all contain similar elements. The use of a frame for lesson planning can serve as a reminder to teachers to consider many of the variables that can influence the success of the lesson. The steps of the lessons can be best crafted through the use of a series of statements. Let's look at seven components of a dynamic lesson (see Form 4.1).

Form 4.1. Sample Lesson Plan Format

Subject: _____   Grade Level: _____

Date: _____   Duration: _____

Learning Objectives:

Content Standards:

Anticipatory Set:

Instruction:

Guided Practice:

Independent Practice:

Assessment and Closure:

Reflection:

"This Is Our Purpose": Learning Objectives and Standards

The first step in lesson planning is to determine the purpose for the lesson. The purpose for a lesson should not be an isolated skill unconnected to other learning, but rather should state in observable and measurable terms exactly what a student will be able to do and how he or she will demonstrate mastery. These learning objectives are best stated through the use of action verbs like *classify* or *estimate*, rather than vague and difficult-to-measure constructs like "understand" or "know." These learning objectives are then used to determine assessment measures of student success. In addition, many schools now require the use of content-area standards in lesson planning to ensure that student experiences match the learning goals of the district and state. Content standards are usually broader than learning objectives, and are often written to encompass instruction that spans an entire grade level. The learning objectives cited in the lesson should advance students toward mastery of the standards. As noted in chapter 1, social and communication objectives for the lesson should be also be considered. Teachers in responsive classrooms know that addressing only content or academic objectives does not facilitate the development of the whole student.

"Here's What We're Doing Today": Anticipatory Set

In order to enhance the learning of students, begin the lesson with a short activity or prompt that will focus their attention. This anticipatory set should "hook" students to the upcoming lesson and alert them to the topic or concept being studied. These activities are brief in nature (one to five minutes), and can include an advance organizer (Ausubel, 1978) to brief students on the day's events. An example of an anticipatory set on the study of volcanoes may be to take the class quickly outside, shake up a can of soda, and watch to see what happens. This is sure to get the attention of your students as they will wonder why the can erupts as it does. Other examples of anticipatory set activities include posting a question related to the day's lesson on the board or reading a story that will prompt discussion and response.

"Let Me Show You": Instruction and Modeling

This phase is the most closely associated with traditional teaching. During instruction, content is explicitly presented to students, and the teacher's level of control is high. Connections between prior knowledge and the new concepts or skills are also taught through the use of graphic organizers, semantic maps, and other strategies. Modeling is interwoven into instruction, and students are shown in a graphic form or through demonstration what the finished product looks like. While instruction and modeling are essential components of a lesson, they are not the end goal. Rather, the purpose is to move students to guided practice, the true heart of a lesson. Photo 4.1 shows a teacher providing instruction during a math lesson.

Photo 4.1. Fifth-Grade Teacher Explicitly Modeling a New Concept

"Follow Me": Guided Practice

The centerpiece of an effective lesson is the progress students achieve when receiving some support. This practice echoes Lev Vygotsky's (1978) theory of "zones of proximal development." Vygotsky theorizes that when children receive support just beyond what they can accomplish independently, they learn new skills and concepts. He defines the zone as "the distance between the actual developmental level as determined by independent problem solving and the level of potential development as determined through problem solving under adult guidance or in collaboration with more capable peers" (1978, p. 86). In guided practice, the teacher leads students through the steps necessary to accomplish the goals of the lesson. This learner experiences the support through a pattern of "see, hear, do." By using the combination of visual, auditory, and kinesthetic support, the learner is able to respond at increasingly higher levels of independence. This continuum provides a sliding scale of support for diverse learners, because students who need more or less support can progress at their own pace. This phase should not be rushed, as it serves as the keystone to the lesson.

"Now You Try It": Independent Practice

At this stage of the lesson, teacher control is further reduced as the learners assume more responsibility. Working independently, or in pairs or small groups, students now practice on their own, applying what they have just been taught. The teacher may circulate and assist, in some cases reteaching in order to clarify understanding (see Photo 4.2.).

"What You've Learned": Assessment and Closure

The end of the lesson is assessment and closure. The purpose of assessment in lesson planning is to gather evidence to determine whether each child has learned what was taught. The learning objectives first outlined at the beginning of the lesson planning process are again used to design the assessment of the lesson. If the learning objective is to

Photo 4.2.   Fifth-Grade Teacher Assisting a Student During Independent Practice

sort words according to their vowel pattern, then the assessment must give students an opportunity to demonstrate this ability. Likewise, if the learning objective is to graph variables on an x and y axis, then the assessment is whether the students performed the operation correctly. An objective for students to determine major causes for the United

States' entry into World War II dictates that the assessment measure products that indicate their ability to articulate reasonable hypotheses about this topic. In all cases, the learning objectives and assessments are tightly related. The use of clearly defined assessment methods in lessons provides to the teacher important information about whether the concepts need to be retaught to individuals, small groups, or the entire class.

Closure signals the students that the lesson is finished. Like an anticipatory set, closure assists students in making connections between prior knowledge and new knowledge. Closure activities are also short in duration, relative to the length of the lesson, and usually consist of a review of the key points of the lesson. An old maxim of teaching still holds true: "Tell them what they'll learn; tell them; then tell them what they learned."

"What Did I Like? What Will I Do Differently?": Reflection

Another key to teaching and learning is reflective practice. Wise practitioners know that engaging in reflection after the lesson serves to constantly improve teacher effectiveness, because it assists teachers in becoming confident professionals. The role of self-reflection and self-analysis has become a critical element in teacher preparation programs (Freese, 1999) and staff development for in-service teachers (Beerens, 2000). Reflective practices often analyze student responses and the teacher's own behaviors. Reflection is best done soon after the lesson is over—within 24 hours, if possible. Recall student responses for evidence of understanding. Were many of the questions of a logistical nature? These may indicate that clearer directions are needed. Did student responses incorporate peers' observations? If not, teaching students how to engage in accountable talk may be in order. Review the teacher behaviors as well. Was the time allotted adequate? Did all students have opportunities to respond? If either of these areas is problematic, the teacher can alter subsequent plans.

CULMINATING PROJECTS

While daily lesson plans have built-in closure activities, they do not signal to students that the unit of study has been completed. Culminating projects are one way that teachers in responsive classrooms meet their goal of gaining closure. Culminating projects are big closure activities that give students opportunities to demonstrate their understanding of the unit's central issue or problem through a product. When teachers provide choices for how students can present their final exhibition, including options for written papers, demonstrations, presentations, and building models, each student has the opportunity to use his or her favored learning style. For example, the students reading *Of Mice and Men* (Steinbeck, 1937) may create a mock trial of George and try him for killing Lenny. Students can be assigned roles such as judge, jury member, lawyers, plaintiff, witnesses, defendant, and print and radio journalists covering the trial. Alternatively, a culminating project focused on the same unit of study could be a visual and written essay focused on "heroes from the Great Depression."

CULMINATING CLASSROOM PROJECTS

The students in Mr. Giaquinto's kindergarten class construct a large mural of life long ago and now. Students draw pictures, paint, and construct the text together through interactive writing in order to explain their mural. During this process, students are consistently negotiating the meaning of what to write and what to display on the poster board.

The students in Ms. Pham-Barron's second-grade class are engaged in several daily activities that lead to the culminating project of writing a personality profile. Some of the daily activities are mapping the story, retelling historical events in small groups, and creating Before-and-After posters of the past and today. For a culminating activity, each student selects to write about a hero who has had an impact on life in the past and today. Students research this hero, create a poster of this hero, and present the information in front of other second-grade classes around the school.

The students in Ms. Allen's fifth-grade class work in groups and study explorers. At the end of the unit, each group presents a skit that they have written about the explorer. They use information from their textbook, informational books from the library, videos, and the Internet to piece together the life experiences of their selected explorer. Each group also creates a test for the members of their class to take after the presentation. Thus, students in Ms. Allen's class take five tests on different explorers!

Throughout the unit, the students in Ms. Mellander's seventh-grade math class review their knowledge of decimals and fractions by playing Bingo games and writing paragraphs about converting decimals into percentages, and complete the unit by filling in a large chart showing decimals and percent values for fractions including numerators and denominators between 1 and 10. Students work in cooperative groups to complete the charts and the finished product is hung in the room for easy reference.

The students in Mr. Hernandez's ninth-grade class walk around the school taking notes on the school and neighborhood surroundings. Students respond often to the poetry they have read and have discussions in whole and small groups. As a culminating project, students draft, revise, and publish a poem or two for the school newspaper or class Publication Poetry book.

In Ms. Grant's high school physics class, students participate in a number of labs (marble momentum, collision, water balloon). Students take notes daily, read from their textbooks and handouts in small groups, and present their findings to the whole class. Students participate in reciprocal teaching where group members use four strategies to make meaning from the text: summarizing, question generating, clarifying, and predicting. See also Table 4.1 for more information.

WHAT DO YOU THINK?

1. Think of an upcoming lesson you will teach. How will you "hook" your students into your lesson and explain briefly what it is that they will be learning?

2. Think about this same lesson or a different one. How will you explicitly teach students the content? How will you change your instruction if your students don't seem to understand the concept the first time?

3. What daily activities and/or culminating projects would fit with a series of lessons you have taught? What materials will students need? How will they be grouped? How will your assessment match what you ask your students to do in the culminating project?

Table 4.1. Standards/Expectations and Essential Questions, Assessments, Materials, and Daily Activities or Culminating Activities

	K	Grade 2	Grade 5	Grade 7	Grade 9	Grades 10–12
Standards/ Expectations and Essential Questions	**Standard: K.6** Students understand that history relates to events, people, and places of other times. **Question:** What are the differences between living today and living long ago?	**Standard: 2.5** Students understand the importance of individual action and character and explain how heroes from long ago and the recent past have made a difference in others' lives. **Question:** How have the actions of others impacted life in the past and today?	**Standard: 5.2** Students trace the routes of early explorers and describe the early explorations of the Americas. **Question:** What were some of the entrepreneurial characteristics of early explorers and the technological developments that made sea exploration possible?	**Standard: 1.5** Students know that every rational number is either a terminating or repeating decimal and can convert terminating decimals into reduced fractions. **Question:** How do we use rational numbers in our everyday lives?	**Standard: 1.2** Students use precise language, action verbs, sensory details, modifiers, active, (not passive) voice. **Question:** What are the sensory details that create imagery in a poem?	**Standard: 2G** Students know how to solve problems involving elastic and inelastic collisions in one dimension by using the principles of conservation of momentum and energy. **Question:** When given the condition for a collision, how can you use the law of conservation of momentum, along with energy equations, to solve for an unknown quantity (such as velocity)?

Assessments	KWL, questioning, anecdotal notes, writing samples with accompanying rubrics	KWL, Venn diagram, questioning, anecdotal notes	KWL, quick write, oral reports, cloze passages, multiple choice test	Unit test, study guides, exit slips, vocabulary quizzes, checklist for daily schoolwork and homework	Journal entries, daily poems, homework, part of final exam	Construction of "egg safety device," written report describing device, momentum problems, momentum exam
Materials	Picture books, videos, photos, realia of clothing, pots and pans, tools, pictures of one-room schoolhouses	Maps, timelines, picture books, famous speeches, videos, social studies textbook.. newspapers	Computer programs, social studies text, maps of the world, compass, picture books, field trip to museum, diaries	Math textbook, teacher-generated notes, Decimal Equivalents activity sheet, math games, math experts	Stacey Tolbert workshop, guest teachers, poems, sensory charts, poetry.com, texts	Cornell notes form, physics textbook, supplemental handouts on momentum, video, picture books
Daily Activities or Culminating Activities	Storyboard, Then-and-Now mural, interactive writing	Mapping the story, class retell, Before-and-After posters, reading travel log, author's study, choral reading, personality profile	Persuasive writing, oral reports, Socratic seminar, shared reading, note taking, RAFT	Decimal and percent chart, Bingo games, written explanations of math concepts	Topic poems (nature, neighborhood, surroundings, emotions), journal entry to poetry writing, Publication Poetry book	Marble momentum lab, note taking, water balloon lab, reciprocal teaching, collision lab, shared reading

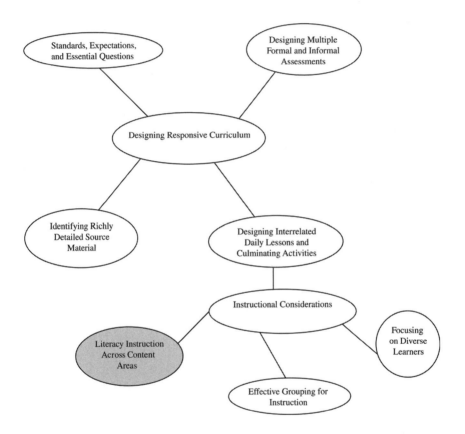

5

LITERACY INSTRUCTION ACROSS CONTENT AREAS

We've all heard the maxim: Students beyond grade 3 move from learning to read to reading to learn. Direct, explicit instruction in decoding is gradually decreased as the content of science, social studies, and mathematics takes on a more prominent role. The amount of text to be read also increases as students progress through the grade levels. The vocabulary requirements continue to grow as well, as readers encounter the technical terminology and discourse of the hard and soft sciences (Lemke, 1990). A result is that the achievement gap accelerates as readers who struggled in the primary grades fall further behind their peers.

This challenge emerges at precisely the time the role of the teacher is changing as well. At the secondary level, teachers increasingly identify themselves by their specialty area. Relatively few have formal experience in teaching reading or writing. And the facts are sobering—while the demands of the technology marketplace require graduates with higher proficiency in reading, students continue to lag behind in their acquisition of critical literacy skills (Barton, 1997).

The reading demands of content-area classes can provide ideal opportunities to develop and extend critical literacy skills using informational text (Farnan, 1996). However, many of the teachers of those very same classes also express dismay at exactly how to accomplish this. A recent study of 435 K–12 teachers showed that fewer than half could identify widely known content-area reading strategies such as KWL (Ogle, 1986), and only 30% actually used it (Spor & Schneider, 1999). Although it is not necessary to transform content-area teachers into reading teachers, it is wise to show them how to infuse defensible literacy strategies into content classes. The remainder of this chapter provides information about the ways in which teachers can infuse literacy instruction into their content. More specifically, this chapter focuses on teaching questioning strategies, discussion strategies to enhance comprehension, textbook feature knowledge, read-alouds, vocabulary development, and writing to learn, which all teachers can use.

TEACHING QUESTIONING STRATEGIES

In many traditional classrooms, questioning was controlled by the teacher, who determined when it would begin and end, what topics would be discussed (and what would not), and the extent to which students would participate. These interchanges often followed a predictable recursive sequence called I-R-E or Initiate-Respond-Evaluate (Cazden, 1986; Mehan, 1979). Students in these classrooms came to expect that the teacher would first initiate a question for a student to respond to, then evaluate the answer for accuracy, and finally follow with another question. In this model, the primary responsibility of the student was to furnish a "correct" answer. Rarely were students welcomed to initiate their own questions or to direct their questions to peers.

At one time, this model dominated classroom conversation in America's schools. Almasi (1995) reported that the I-R-E sequence comprised 85% of the discussions in her study's fourth-grade classrooms! Importantly, the I-R-E pattern of teacher-student interchange rarely allows for the critical higher order thinking associated with meaningful learning (Kuhn, 1999). The modeling of these teacher-led questioning patterns furthers the internal questioning students engage in when they read, and values factual knowledge over synthesis and evaluation.

Teachers in responsive curriculum classrooms explicitly teach questioning strategies to foster critical thinking in their students. This encourages students to take an active role in their own learning because they consciously employ these strategies to better comprehend the text and the concepts it is presenting. Two widely taught strategies are Question-Answer Relationship (Raphael, 1986) and Question the Author (Beck, McKeown, Worthy, Sandora, & Kucan, 1993). These techniques support student inquiry into the deeper levels of meaning to be found in narrative and informational text.

Question-Answer Relationship (Raphael, 1986), also known as QAR, is a framework to forward students' understanding of the text-explicit and text-implicit information in their readings (Lapp & Flood, 1992). In the case of Right There and Think and Search questions, for example, students refer to one or more locations in the text for the answers. This contrasts with On My Own and Author and You questions that require students to access their background knowledge and experiences. These questions are given to students in advance of a reading to better orient them to the information they should anticipate in the text. It also models what fluent readers already know—that reading is a transaction between both the text and what the reader brings to the text. In addition to identifying types of questions, students are also charged with creating questions for use in small-group discussions. When students are made aware of these different structures in expository text, their writing and comprehension improves (Raphael, Engler, & Kirschner, 1986).

In another questioning strategy that supports literacy development, Question the Author, students read narrative and informational text closely while analyzing the author's intent in the messages carried by the words. Three basic queries are initiated by asking these questions:

1. What is the author trying to say here?
2. What is the author's message?
3. What is the author talking about? (Beck, McKeown, Hamilton, & Kucan, 1997, p. 35)

By asking questions like these, the teacher can move students beyond discrete facts to the larger ideas and concepts held in passages. Discussion centers around the text, rather than on memorized facts. These queries are advantageous because they prompt longer and more detailed student responses while constructing the meaning built through successive sentences, paragraphs, and chapters (Beck, McKeown, Hamilton, & Kucan, 1997). They also emphasize the voice and point of view held in any author's work, a vital skill necessary for critical analysis of information.

DISCUSSION STRATEGIES TO ENHANCE COMPREHENSION

As beads are to a necklace, so is questioning to a discussion. One of the outcomes of teaching questioning strategies is that the questions can be extended into meaningful classroom discourse. Students often have difficulty interpreting the dense informational text found in textbooks (Martin, Van Cleaf, & Hodges, 1988), and discussion can help learners synthesize their prior knowledge with the new pieces of data. In this model, students construct meaning through connections to themselves, to other information sources, and to the larger world around them. As students read, they can interact with the text, using Post-it notes to identify when they are making a connection to their own lives (T-S for Text to Self), a connection to another text (T-T for Text to Text), or a connection to the world (T-W for Text to World). (See Photo 5.1.)

Photo 5.1.   Student Using Post-It Notes to Enhance Comprehension

This constructivist approach values the contributions of peers in making meaning (Saunders, 1992). Effective classroom discussions place students at the center in partner and group discussions, with the teacher serving as facilitator. This is not to say that teachers allow the conversation to go in whatever direction it may. On the contrary; effective facilitation of classroom discussion demands the use of thoughtful declarative and reflective statements (Mazzoni & Gambrell, 1996) to seed the discussion and guide it when it wanders off course.

Reciprocal teaching (Palincsar & Brown, 1986) brings together questioning strategies and peer-supported learning through large- and small-group discussion. In reciprocal teaching, four comprehension activities—generating questions, summarizing, predicting, and clarifying—are taught within the context of a text passage. The teacher first models each of these stages, then turns the responsibility over to students. Students work in small groups of three to five members to move through the sequence (see Form 5.1). Students take turns in the role of the "teacher" or instructional leader for the small group. As students become more proficient with reciprocal teaching, they may assume a specific role, like "clarifier" or "summarizer." After completing the assigned passage, the classroom teacher once again facilitates a large-group discussion of the reading, using the questions generated by the small groups. Reciprocal teaching has advantages over traditional direct explanation because it fosters procedures fluent readers use (Hermann, 1998) and allows students to capitalize on the contributions of peers to enhance their own understanding.

Effective classroom discussion is dependent on the teacher to create opportunities for content conversations to occur, as in providing reciprocal teaching events. However, some students, particularly English-language learners, have difficulty with inserting themselves into the discussion. They may fear ridicule from peers or lack the habits of mind necessary for formulating a persuasive position and then sharing it with others. These students can benefit from a method of capturing a student's opinions before the discussion begins, as in the use of a discussion web.

A discussion web (Alvermann, 1991) is a graphic organizer for supporting the development and refinement of a student's opinion about a

Form 5.1.   Reciprocal Teaching Discussion Frame

Before Reading:
Select a teacher and a recorder for this passage. The teacher will lead this portion of the reading.
The title of this passage is _____
Predictions for this reading: _____

_____

During the Reading:
Read each paragraph (individually or partnered), then ask a question about the content. Answer each question as a group.

Paragraph	Question	Answer
1		
2		
3		
4		
5		

After the Reading:
Discuss and write a consensus of a summary for this reading.

_____
_____
_____
_____

Discuss any confusing words or phrases.

Confusing Word or Phrase	What We Think It Means

Next Rotation:
Select another member of the group for the role of teacher and recorder. Begin reading the next five paragraphs of the passage.

topic. It combines an organizational chart with a Think-Pair-Share (Slavin, 1989) cooperative learning process (Mazzoni & Gambrell, 1996). The teacher first presents an intriguing question to the students (one that does not have a simple yes/no answer). A worksheet for capturing ideas is distributed to each learner (see Form 5.2). Students first

Form 5.2.

Central Question

Think ...

YES   NO

Pair ...   Some ideas I heard from my partner ...

Share ...   Some further ideas I heard from my class ...

formulate an individual response, then pair with another classmate to begin a discussion on the focus question. Finally, the teacher invites a large-group discussion of the question and records class responses on a similarly formatted chart.

In Ms. Ali's ninth-grade social studies class, students use discussion webs to support their conversation about regulation of the U.S.–Mexico border. In this community, the nearby border is a source of much heated conversation, and many students have family members living on both sides. The teacher has been reading aloud the book *The Circuit*, by Francisco Jimenez (1996), which tells the story of a young boy and his family surviving as migrant farm workers in central California. She first poses the question, Should the U.S. government make it more difficult for people to enter the United States? and then has students write their impressions supporting both sides of the debate. After composing their own thoughts, students are paired to begin a discussion. In addition to sharing their own opinions, they record new responses forwarded by their peers. After a few minutes of paired discussion, Ms. Ali invites a class discussion of the question. She records their thoughts on chart paper, while students note further salient remarks. Ms. Ali later references the class discussion web during their study of the history of immigration policy in the United States, noting the various arguments forwarded to support or defeat immigration legislation. She later remarks that the use of discussion webs is beneficial because it requires students to note opinions that dissented from their own, and provides a structure for English-language learners to support their conversations.

TEXTBOOK FEATURE KNOWLEDGE

In primary grades, students are exposed to a rich level of narrative text. Teachers plan instructional opportunities to discuss story frames; identify the beginning, middle, and end; and analyze characters. Students are frequently asked to retell the story in an effort to clarify understanding and gauge comprehension. However, their experiences with informational text are often limited. As noted earlier, entry into the intermediate grades marks a major shift in the type of text that is used. The importance of narrative text is increasingly balanced with the need to teach content knowledge through informational (expository) text. Yet many students have never received explicit instruction in how to access these textbooks. As with narrative, they require a deliberate and thoughtful effort to acquaint them with the strategies needed to fully extract the information lying in the pages of the textbook.

The genre of informational text differs significantly from narrative text. In addition to the dimensions discussed above, a major point of variance is the nonlinear nature of expository text (Alexander & Jetton, 2000). Unlike stories, which possess a clear time order, science and mathematics textbooks rarely possess a chronological order. Instead, they are usually constructed in a conceptual order. Readers unfamiliar with this difference in genre will approach a textbook like a story and miss the important concepts and major ideas being advanced. Indeed, it has been demonstrated that instruction in the differences in genres leads to improved student learning (Goldman & Rakestraw, 2000).

The structure of the language of the text also poses a problem for less fluent readers. Readers often expect that the first sentence of each paragraph will be the main idea (Baumann, 1986), but this is not always the case in textbooks. Depending on the nature of the author's writing style, a particular textbook may demand specific instruction on identifying the main idea. Informational text also relies more heavily on "pointer words"—the transition words that emphasize key points in the text. Examples of pointer words and phrases include *first, finally, however, in summary*, and *in other words* (Goldman & Rakestraw, 2000). These signaling devices do not contribute to the content itself, but rather are meant to direct the reader's attention to the important concepts. Instructional time devoted to identifying and interpreting pointer words and phrases can increase a reader's ability to comprehend the text, because it provides a language structure for ordering the information. An ironic note is that many so-called remedial textbooks eliminate these pointer words in a misguided effort to shorten sentences to reach a reduced readability quotient for struggling learners (Ciborowski, 1992).

Text features are another distinction in informational text. Narrative works rarely contain headings and subheadings, while most textbooks use these to cue readers to important topic shifts. Pictures, diagrams, and graphs are another text feature unique to expository text. While pictures are often used in stories, they only reflect the action being told by the story. In contrast, many textbooks use these items with captions to convey content. New or unfamiliar vocabulary is also introduced differently in textbooks. For instance, these words may appear in bold or italicized print, and in some textbooks a pronunciation key is also included. And, of course, most textbooks feature organizational elements like a table of contents, glossary, and index. But without instruction and modeling in how to use these, many readers fail to fully comprehend.

Explicit teaching of textbook structures is warranted in all content-area classes. An excellent introduction to a new text is a book walk and scavenger hunt. A book walk is a simple lesson on the features of the textbook. Students are introduced to the major organizational features like the table of contents and index. The teacher orients the class to the

Form 5.3. Scavenger Hunt

Science Textbook Treasure Hunt

Group Members: _____

Title of Textbook: _____

Organization

What textbook feature tells the reader the titles and pages of the chapters?
_____

This textbook has _____ chapters.

The glossary gives word definitions and is on pages _____ to _____.

The _____ is in the back of the book and tells the reader on what page a word can be found.

Text Features

Turn to Chapter 2. What is the title? _____

List the first three headings (they are in bold capital letters). _____
_____

List the sixth, seventh, and eighth subheadings (they are in bold lowercase letters).
_____ _____ _____

How many photographs are in this chapter? _____

How many charts and graphs? _____ How many drawings?_____

Make a prediction about what you expect to learn in this chapter.
_____
_____

Scavenger Hunt: On what page would you find ...

Information about satellites   _____

A photograph of a boa constrictor   _____

A diagram of the food chain   _____

A description of the Challenger accident   _____

A question about tectonic plates   _____

Who Wants to Be a Science Millionaire?

Use your textbook to find the answers to these questions:

The name of the green substance found in plant leaves   _____

The pronunciation for the word "Sputnik"   _____

The year of the San Francisco earthquake   _____

The names of five simple machines

_____ _____

_____ _____

_____

Form 5.3. *(continued)*

This textbook uses words and phrases to tell you when something important is coming. Some examples are *first, second, third, last, finally, in summary, in other words,* and *for example.* Turn to any chapter that interests you, and find five of these "signal words" that tell a reader to pay attention. Write the page number, too.

Chapter Title: _____

Signal Word	Page Number
_____	_____
_____	_____
_____	_____
_____	_____
_____	_____

Too Cool for School
Here are two things we found in this textbook that look pretty cool:
_____
_____

When You're Finished
Bring this to Ms. Chu and collect your treasure!

structure of the textbook and interesting pictures and diagrams. After conducting a similar book walk, Ms. Chu, a fifth-grade science teacher, held a textbook scavenger hunt (see Form 5.3). Students were paired, and Ms. Chu used the opportunity to observe students to determine their problem-solving skills when using informational text. She says the event was such a success that she plans on using a similar activity to search for resources on the Internet.

READ-ALOUDS

In many schools, read-alouds are done each day, in all content areas, at all grade levels. While this can initially prove to be a stretch for some content teachers, they quickly warm to the idea when they learn of the benefits to learners. Of particular importance is the positive effect read-alouds have on attitudes and motivation toward reading (Worthy & Hoffman, 1999), and especially toward reading nonfiction (Dreher, 1998–1999). It has been shown to be effective in foreign language instruction (Richardson, 1997–1998), social studies (Irvin, Lunstrum, Lynch-Brown, & Shepard, 1995), and mathematics (Richardson, 1997–1998). Read-alouds also support language acquisition for English-language learners (Amer, 1997) because it provides fluent language role models.

One of the first myths in need of squelching is the mistaken notion that read-alouds can only involve narrative text (Vacca, Vacca, Prosenjak, & Burkey, 1996). While fiction and poetry can be effective additions to a content-area class, they should only be used when there is an instructional rationale for using them. Mrs. Aguilar, an eighth-grade social studies teacher, reads aloud the chapter book *Number the Stars* (Lowry, 1989), a moving story of a young Danish girl whose family helps Jews escape Nazi Germany in 1943. "I find that the students relate more closely to the story of Anne Marie [the protagonist] because she's their age. Our study of World War II seems more relevant to them because they've heard the fear in Anne Marie's story."

Other teachers use magazine articles, textbook passages, and newspaper clippings related to their content areas. Mr. Armstead, a sixth-grade math teacher, used daily newspaper stories of the 2000 election vote recounts in Florida to bring the topic of statistics to life. "It just seemed like a great opportunity to show my students the importance of accurate data collection. Every day, the story continued to unfold, and I was able to create some terrific connections with the study of probability. Because the kids asked for it, we even measured the likelihood of arriving at the same figure twice when we counted and then recounted the seeds in hundreds of seed packets." A second-grade teacher reads *Martin's Big Words* (Rappaport, 2001) when studying the Civil Rights Movement and states that "this text infuses accounts of history with Martin Luther King's speeches in order to make history come alive. The students love this book because they can really understand what King's speeches meant for all Americans."

Although the possibilities in incorporating read-alouds are vast, here are a few tips when using read-alouds for content-area instruction.

1. Read-alouds do not need to be long to be effective. A short, powerful passage has far more impact than a long, dull reading. Plan on about five minutes a day, and increase gradually as your students' stamina for listening improves.
2. Practice your read-aloud in advance. Remember that the goal is to provide a fluent language model. That requires a bit of rehearsal so that you can bring the proper expression and inflection to the text. Think of it as a bit of a performance—you wouldn't go on stage without practicing, would you?
3. Choose readings that are meaningful to you and are connected with the course content. Comprehension increases when connections are made, so don't assume that your students understand the relevance of your selection. Be explicit about how you see the information from the selected reading fitting into your course of study.
4. Determine in advance where you're going to stop. Look for the natural breaks in a piece. Selected passages can either be read in a single reading or extended over a few class periods. If the reading will continue on another day, stop at a point where you can elicit predictions about what is yet to come.

The use of read-alouds for content-area instruction models the importance of reading in all aspects of learning. In addition, it delivers information in a format that is accessible to all learners, because it circumvents the variable of a student's independent reading level. Finally, it allows content-area teachers to connect their discipline to the world around them, thereby demonstrating to students the relevance of their study.

VOCABULARY DEVELOPMENT

By some estimates, students acquire 3,000 new words per year (Bryant, Ugel, Hamff, & Thompson, 1999). Nagy and Anderson (1984) estimate that students are exposed to 88,500 words during their school career, far too many to teach through direct instruction. And, as many teachers can attest, a student's limited vocabulary is a major barrier to his or her comprehension of concepts and content. Students with impoverished vocabulary struggle with reading material, are limited in participating in oral language activities, and produce less sophisticated writing. These aspects of learning are keystones in any content-area class; thus, infusing vocabulary and word study into lessons supports acquisition of content. However, logic dictates that the sheer volume makes the teaching of words in isolation impractical. Instead, vocabulary instruction needs to occur within context, and with a goal of helping students form their own connections, or schema, to develop a deeper understanding of the meanings conveyed by a word. Vocabulary development within the context of responsive curriculum includes word sorts, semantic feature analysis, and technical vocabulary building.

The use of word sorts often begins in primary classrooms as a way of supporting an emergent reader's word acquisition. Bear, Templeton, Invernizzi, and Johnson (1996) define word sorts as "an active process in which students categorize words" (p. 66). Students are provided with a series of pictures or words written on index cards, slips of paper, or Post-it notes. In a closed sort, the teacher provides a list of categories and instructs students to place words in the correct category. Mr. Collier uses the following closed word sort during his kindergarten study of animals:

LAND	WATER	AIR
giraffe	fish	eagle
dog	whale	owl
elephant		hummingbird
lion		

Ms. Eagan uses the following closed word sort during her ninth-grade geography class's study of Asia:

JAPAN	CHINA	VIETNAM	PHILIPPINES
yen	Changjiang	Khmer	peso
Tokyo	Beijing	Tran Du	Manila
Peace	Great Wall	Luong	Tagolog
Memorial	Forbidden	Mekong	Joseph Estrada
Akihito	City	Ho Chi Minh	
		City	

She then has the students re-sort the words using new categories:

LEADERS	RIVERS	CURRENCY	CITIES	FAMOUS SITES	LANGUAGE
Tran Du	Changjiang	yen	Tokyo	Great Wall	Tagolog
Long	Mekong	peso	Beijing	Peace	
Akihito			Manila	Memorial	
Joseph			Ho Chi		
Estrada			Minh		
			City		
			Forbidden		
			City		

Ms. Eagan finds that when students have opportunities to reconceptualize characteristics of vocabulary words, they develop a deeper understanding of the words, as evidenced by their written and class discussion work.

Mr. Loaiza, a sixth-grade math teacher, uses an open sort during the first week of math in order to assess his students' understanding of mathematical concepts. An open sort differs from a closed sort in that no categories are furnished to the student; instead, each student constructs categories based on their understanding of the words. He presents students with the following mathematical terms, listed on small slips of paper and placed in an envelope:

Add	Subtract	Multiply	Divide
Product	Sum	Sum	Difference
Algebra	Arithmetic	Geometry	Negative
Angle	Circle	Acute	Prime
Zero	Perimeter	Triangle	Fraction

Mr. Loaiza circulates among the students as they work, pausing to chat with them about their reasons for categorizing terms as they do. He makes notes of each student's insights into their mathematical knowledge, and also collects each student's sorting work and their rationale for choosing their sorts. The teacher does this at the beginning of each year because he finds that his students are more relaxed about explaining their thinking than during a traditional test. "Lots of kids freeze up when the teacher says, 'OK, everyone clear off your desks and take out a pencil.' But when I have them do activities like word sorts and then talk with them about their reasoning, I get more feedback. It's like I can see their wheels turning. You can't get that from a multiple choice quiz."

Like word sorts, semantic feature analysis helps students categorize the characteristics of words in relation to one another (Anders & Bos, 1986). Students work from a grid of vocabulary words and features. Intersecting squares that represent a true statement are filled in with a plus (+), while those that do not possess that feature are given a minus (−). Semantic feature analysis grids can be further expanded to include other categories as well. Sixth-grade teacher Mrs. Ross used this semantic feature analysis during her social studies unit on the history of peace (see Form 5.4).

Students used this grid throughout the unit, adding historical and modern examples as they discovered them in their course of study. Mrs. Ross said the purpose of this semantic feature analysis was not to ensure that students generated a single "right" answer, but rather that they constructed and defined their own meaning. When they neared the end of the unit, she invited them to discuss their selections in groups of five. "That was a real lesson in peace for all of them! They had to listen to other people's ideas, even if they didn't agree with them. They got a firsthand experience at 'patience' and 'tolerance'!"

As Mrs. Ross noted, the true power of word sorts and semantic feature analysis is the personal investment students make in defining words

---

Form 5.4. Semantic Feature Analysis

WORD	CONTRIBUTES TO PEACE	THREATENS PEACE	HISTORICAL EXAMPLE	CURRENT EXAMPLE
Tolerance	+	−		
Respect	+	−	Ghandi	
Prejudice	−	+		Milosevic
Bigotry	−	+	Hitler	
Patience	+	−		
Scorn	−	+		
Rapport	+	−	Eleanor Roosevelt	
Conflict	− or +	− or +		

(Ruddell, 1996). By revisiting their work at sorts and semantic feature analyses, they deepen their understanding of the words and their uses.

The technical meanings of some vocabulary words can be a bewildering maze for some learners, and especially for those who are acquiring English as a second or third language. How can "ruler" mean one thing in history and another in math (West, 1978)? As students enter the intermediate grades, the demands for the use and understanding of technical terms increases. In mathematics, students encounter words like *prime*, *product*, and *operation*, and all require a very specific usage. Science carries an even more technical vocabulary. Words in a seventh-grade science chapter about the human body included words like *tissue*, *organ*, and *vessel*. These words, and many others, carry both a common and a technical meaning. But how can we help create these connections?

A simple system used in content-area classrooms is the vocabulary notebook. In each class, students devote a section of their notebook to a vocabulary table. Through the semester, vocabulary words are recorded, along with both their common and technical definitions. A source notation is also included so that the students can refer back to an example of the word in their readings.

While Mr. Armstead, a sixth-grade math teacher, used the election as a way to connect students to statistical concepts, his teaching partner, Ms. Anaya, used the vocabulary notebook in her social studies class. "Mr. Armstead was doing lots of read-alouds from the newspaper on the unfolding developments in Florida, but they contained lots of legal vocabulary that was new to my students. So we began collecting the common and technical definitions of the words in our notebooks. Pretty soon we had a great chart of new words." Here is a student sample (see form 5.5).

The notebooks were helpful in Mr. Armstead's class because he could refer students back to their notes when a newly acquired word was used in his read-alouds. When an unknown word was used, students entered it into their vocabulary notebooks for later discussion with the social studies teacher. "It was really interdisciplinary in the best sense of the word," reflected Mr. Armstead.

Form 5.5.   Vocabulary Journal

VOCABULARY WORD	COMMON DEFINITION	TECHNICAL DEFINITION	SOURCE
party	A celebration	A political organization (Democratic, Republican, Green)	Pg. 38, social studies book
motion	To move	To ask for something in a court	Article on Florida courts
hearing	To detect a sound	A court procedure to listen to both sides of an argument	Worksheet
landmark	A famous place	A court case that decides something new	Newspaper article from 11/19/00
right	A direction or side	In politics, a person with conservative beliefs	Ms. Anaya
left	The other direction	In politics, a person with liberal beliefs	Ms. Anaya
moderate	Not too much and not too little— just right	In politics, someone who's in the middle	Ms. Anaya
chad	A boy's name	The little paper square that you poke out on a ballot	Magazine article from 11/23/00

WRITING TO LEARN

The writing-to-learn strategy can be utilized across academic content areas (e.g., Andrews, 1997; Prain & Hand, 1996). This brief strategy (10 minutes or so) is introduced as a prompt, phrased as a question or sentence starter. The student spends a few minutes formulating a response, then writes for five or so minutes. Writing to learn should not be used as a summary of facts and sequences, but rather as a way to engage the learners in reflection as they make meaning of new material by having them apply what they have learned to a new situation.

Mr. Simon uses writing to learn in his science class to provide students an opportunity to focus on the lesson for the day and to transition from their hectic passing periods between classes. While studying the respiratory system, he invites students to write in their journals about the flow of air from outside the body, through the nose or mouth, and to the blood supply.

Another writing to learn activity is called RAFT—role, audience, format, and topic (Santa & Havens, 1995). More specifically, RAFT means the following (Santa, Havens, & Harrison, 1996, p. 175):

1. The role of the writer (Who is the writer?)
2. The audience (To whom are you writing?)
3. The format (What form will it take?)
4. The topic and strong verb (What is your topic and verb?)

In traditional writing assignments, students write for the teacher as the primary audience member. RAFT assignments allow the teacher to vary any of the four dimensions of writing, which makes the writing task far more interesting for students. For example, in the science class, students may arrive from passing period and see the following on the board:

R—the respiratory system
A—oxygen
F—love letter
T—why I need you

The same students may leave their science class and arrive in their humanities class and see the following on the board:

if your last name starts with A–M	if your last name starts with N–Z
R—American colonist	R—British colonist
A—King George III	A—George Washington
F—protest letter	F—protest letter
T—Set us free	T—You belong to us

When students are first introduced to RAFT writing, the teacher provides more specific information. Over time, students will complete their RAFT assignments independently. Teachers can use RAFT as an opening for a new unit of study or as a culminating writing assignment to assess student knowledge about the topic.

Let's return to our six teachers and see how they have used effective literacy instruction while students engage in daily content-area activities (as shown in Table 5.1).

In Mr. G's kindergarten class, students read a big book as a shared reading. The text, *Wheel Away* (Dodds, 1989) is displayed on a big book stand so all students have access to the print and illustrations. Prior to reading the text, Mr. G introduces key vocabulary through flashcards (mill, pig pens, tar) and brings in realia so students can see and feel some of the words with which they may have been unfamiliar. Mr. G reads the patterned text several times. When comfortable, students begin to choral-read the text with the teacher. Students are able to retell the events of the story by using the flashcards, realia, and illustrations from the text.

Ms. Pham-Barrons reads aloud *A Picture Book of Rosa Parks* (Adler, 1995) to her second-grade class. While reading, Ms. Pham-Barron models a think-aloud in which she stops periodically throughout the text to share with the students what she is thinking. Ms. Pham-Barron thinks out loud and says, "I wonder how Rosa Parks was feeling when she sat down on the bus? I know sometimes when I am tired I just can't even move a muscle. I wonder if that is how she felt." About halfway through the text, Ms. Pham-Barron calls on a couple of students to share with the class what they are thinking about the text. By the end of the text, because the teacher has modeled what continuous comprehension monitoring may sound like and because several students have shared their thoughts, students are ready to share their thoughts with a partner. The teacher models how a retell of the story may sound and students practice orally sharing their own retell with a partner before composing a written retell.

Ms. Allen believes in explicit instruction, teacher modeling, guided practice, and continuous monitoring to ensure students become fluent writers. Prior to writing, students read examples of persuasive writing and talk about this genre while charting the components. Ms. Allen asks her students to write a three-paragraph persuasive essay in which they are to assume the role of an explorer asking the king or queen for money for their voyage. With the help of her students, Ms. Allen uses the overhead projector to model how the first paragraph may be written. In pairs, students construct the second paragraph attending to the components of a persuasive essay. Students are now ready to write the third paragraph on their own. Ms. Allen monitors her writers and individually conferences with them. Students refer to content-area word walls, thesauruses, and previously read texts for resources.

Ms. Mellander wants her students to explain the conversion of decimals into percents in written form. In order to do so, students brainstorm a list of words that they have been using orally and reading about in order to explain the process (convert, numerator, denominator, fraction, reduce). Ms. Mellander models for the class how to understand tricky vocabulary words more thoroughly through a word map. Ms. Mellander draws a graphic organizer on the overhead projector and explains how each word needs to have a definition, synonym, illustration, and sentence. After modeling the first word, students work in pairs creating word maps for the other words. Now students are ready to use this vocabulary for their written responses in which they explain how to convert a decimal into a percentage.

In order to assess whether students understood the poem "Holes" by Lillian Morrison (from *This Place I Know* [Heard, 2002]), students were asked to write RAFTs in their journals. This poem, along with several others, were read on the second anniversary of 9/11. Several discussions about the writer's role, audience, format, and topic have occurred in Mr. Hernandez's ninth-grade class. Students were ready to write to the following RAFT as they increased their comprehension of the poem:

R – a survivor
A – firefighter
F – thank you letter
T – How you saved my life

Students were grouped in fives after writing in order to share their work and discuss different perspectives and writing styles.

In order to understand the concept of momentum more clearly, Ms. Grant groups her physics students in fours, assigning each one of

Table 5.1. Daily Activities or Culminating Activities and Literacy Instruction

	K	Grade 2	Grade 5	Grade 7	Grade 9	Grades 10–12
Daily Activities or Culminating Activities	Storyboard, Then-and-Now mural, interactive writing	Mapping the story, class retell, Before-and-After posters, reading travel log, author's study, choral reading, personality profile	Persuasive writing, oral reports, Socratic seminar, shared reading, note taking, RAFT	Decimal and percent chart, Bingo games, written explanations of math concepts	Topic poems (nature, neighborhood, surroundings, emotions), journal entry to poetry writing, Publication Poetry book	Marble momentum lab, note taking, water balloon lab, reciprocal teaching, collision lab, shared reading
Literacy Instruction	Introduce key vocabulary words through flashcards and realia. Using a big book, the teacher models reading and students join in when prompted.	Teacher models a "think-aloud." Students share ideas with a partner, then share out to whole class. Students use content area word wall as they retell information.	In pairs, students read a few examples of persuasive writing. Together, the teacher and students construct a paragraph. Students complete the next paragraph in pairs and the third paragraph independently.	Use word map for new vocabulary in which students must define the word, write a synonym, illustrate, use in a sentence.	Students "power write" and practice generative sentences. After reading poems individually and as a shared reading, students complete RAFTs.	In groups of four, students engage in reciprocal teaching in which each student assumes the role of summarizer, question generator, clarifyer, and predictor. Notes for each role are taken in a journal and roles and journals are shared regularly.

them a role: summarizer, question generator, clarifyer, and predictor. While first reading a handout on momentum independently, each student takes notes in his or her journal. After the initial reading, students volunteers to read the handout a second time, this time pausing while the student "teachers" summarize what is read, ask questions, clarify confusing paragraphs, and make predictions related to the topic. Ms. Grant switches roles and student members often to ensure all students are participating and utilizing comprehension strategies.

CONCLUSION

Ensuring that students can assess the text and understand the content of class discussions is vital. Teachers who use responsive curriculum design methods also understand that they can infuse literacy instruction into their teaching. While teachers do not address each of these instructional strategies each time they plan a lesson, over time students do experience them all. For example, all students should hear every one of their teachers read aloud regularly. Literacy is an access skill that all students must have to successfully enter the adult world. By ensuring both content knowledge and literacy skill development, teachers ensure student success.

WHAT DO YOU THINK?

1. Think about a text you have read to your class. What did you do to ensure students understood any confusing or technical vocabulary words?
2. In most classrooms there exists a wide range of literacy proficiencies. What do you do to ensure that your emerging readers can comprehend what they are reading? How do you challenge your most fluent readers?
3. Think of your classroom environment. How can you create a print-rich environment with many literacy resources?

6

EFFECTIVE GROUPING
FOR INSTRUCTION

In the United States, grouping for instruction has been dominated by a tradition of fixed ability grouping (Dewey, 1939/1998; Dreeben & Barr, 1988; Flood, Lapp, Flood, & Nagel, 1992; Haller, 1985; Powell & Hornsby, 1993; Slavin, 1990; Soderman, Gregory, & O'Neill, 1999). In the traditional classrooms of the past, these homogeneous grouping patterns were tied to myriad difficulties, including social, emotional, and learning problems for students (e.g., DeVries & Edwards, 1974; Haller & Davis, 1980; Hiebert, 1983; Johnson, Johnson, & Maruyama, 1983; McKerrow, 1997; Spear, 1994). In order to minimize the negative effects of static grouping practices, educators and researchers have designed flexible grouping patterns (e.g., Cunningham, Hall, & Defee, 1998; Fields & Spangler, 1995; Heuwinkel, 1996; Lapp, Flood, & Ranck-Buhr, 1997). In these flexible grouping patterns, homogeneous groups are still sometimes used—but strategically, for specific instructional purposes (Indrisano & Paratore, 1991; Prawat, 1999; Swing & Peterson, 1982).

Flexible grouping practices provide a menu of patterns for teachers to implement. Whole-group instruction, possibly the most prevalent configuration used in classrooms, is viewed as just one option for teaching and learning. Whole-group instruction is particularly useful when introducing new material, or at the beginning of a new unit of instruction. For example, when beginning a unit on folktales, the teacher may begin by reading several folktales to the entire class and having whole-group discussions about the features of folktales. Similarly, when opening a new unit on 3-D design in art, the teacher uses whole-group instruction to show a collection of slides on notable collage, mixed media, and sculpture entries from the previous year's annual exhibition. But whole-group instruction is limited in its effectiveness, and other configurations are necessary if the teacher is going to meet the needs of all students in today's diverse classrooms (Gamoran, 1989; Lipton & Hubble, 1997; Opitz, 1992; Slavin, 1996). The art teacher knows that other patterns are available, and uses a series of questions to make decisions about how to strategically employ both heterogeneous (mixed) and homogeneous (same) groups.

QUESTIONS TO ASK WHEN GROUPING

1. What are the goals and objectives for the lesson?
   The goals of the lesson are the first factor in determining the best possible grouping pattern. As mentioned above, whole-group instruction may work best for an introduction to a new concept or unit. However, subsequent instruction to deepen students' understanding requires small-group and partnered explorations. Thus, the goals and objectives tie the lesson plan to the grouping pattern.
2. What comprises the students' background knowledge?
   A teacher may first select a whole-group pattern in order to lead a conversation with students to determine the levels of knowledge they bring to a new unit or concept. Later, homogeneous groups with student experts having in-depth topical knowledge can lead small-group activities. This facilitates a shared learning experience, while promoting a student-centered classroom.
3. What is the range of student fluency in oral language?
   Students who are acquiring English-language proficiency benefit greatly from opportunities to hone their growing skills with peers. In responsive curriculum classrooms, teachers carefully place these students into small groups with a language broker who can mediate understanding within the group and provide corrective feedback.
4. What are students' interests and work habits?
   Students possess a wide range of work habits. Some prefer working alone; others are content allowing peers to take the lead. Some

students have a strong interest in the topic of study; others are only interested in completing the unit and moving on to another topic. Careful mixing of students with diverse work habits and interests creates an opportunity for modeling. These groups need careful monitoring to ensure both individual and group success.

5. Are there social concerns or needs?

A teacher may have a social reason for mixing a group of leaders and followers, talkers and quiet students. In such a group, each student has the chance to both receive and provide modeling for the others. These interpersonal and communication skills are reinforced through the use of group roles (recorder, spokesperson, materials manager, cheerleader) that play sometimes to a student's strengths and at other times to his or her area of need.

6. Do students have a choice?

At times, allowing for student choice in the selection of a partner or small group provides encouragement in accepting responsibility for their performance and work patterns. Before introducing student choice as one of the grouping configurations, create classroom community expectations that ensure that no student can be excluded or stranded without a group.

7. What are appropriate grouping formats?

The six common types of group configurations include individuals, dyads or pairs, small groups of three or four students, large groups of seven to eight students, half class groups of 15 or so, and whole-class grouping (Cohen, 1986, 1994; Flood et al., 1992; Reutzel, 1999; Worthy & Hoffman, 1996). These groups can be student-directed, led by the teacher, or a combination of both.

8. What materials are available?

The demands of a particular activity may necessitate that a particular group of students work together to access the same materials. Leveled text, in the form of books, magazine articles, and other sources, ensures participation by all the group's members. When reading for information gathering, it is vital that students have access to text that is at their independent reading level. Text can be easily leveled by the teacher using the Fry Readability Scale (Fry, 1969). However, it is not necessary (or advisable) to place students in groups solely according to their reading levels. By creating activities and providing a wide range of leveled text, each member of the group can seek source material written at his or her independent reading level and then return to the group with the information acquired. Thus, the emphasis shifts from reading as a purpose to reading for a purpose.

The amount of materials available can also dictate a grouping pattern. Most classrooms and school libraries possess a limited number of books on a particular topic. This can be circumvented by creating small "expert groups" to research a single aspect of a broader topic, as was done in one ninth-grade science class studying the Amazon rain forest. Each group studied one issue affecting the rain forest, including deforestation, the rights of indigenous people, natural resources, current political tensions, and the biodiversity of the region. The groups then reconstituted as heterogeneous knowledge groups, with each member teaching the others about his or her topic. The use of this "jigsaw" method (Aronson, 2000) maximized finite resource materials while creating a common knowledge base on a complex topic.

Answers to these and similar questions help to provide a basis for the grouping configurations that best support instruction designed to meet students' needs. Let's take a look inside three classrooms as these various grouping configurations are implemented (e.g., Lapp, Fisher, Flood, Geiss, & Flood, 1999).

CLASSROOM ORGANIZATION OF FLEXIBLE GROUPING PATTERNS

Welcome to Kumeyaay Middle School. Students at Kumeyaay are organized into academic families of four content teachers—English, social studies, science, and math. A total of 125 students stay with their four "family" teachers throughout their middle school experience. In addition to classes taught by these four teachers, students attend a number of visual and performing arts classes over their three years in middle school. These discovery classes are sequenced according to the curriculum in sixth, seventh, and eighth grade.

We join the students of House C as they study natural disasters. Each of the teachers in House C is using the theme of natural disasters to organize the curriculum. The students have been told that they are in the middle of an emergency. They know that a major tropical depression has formed off the coast of West Africa. Will the storm intensify into a hurricane? Will it threaten valuable shipping lanes and the vulnerable southeast coastline of the United States? Should an evacuation notice be issued? Let's look inside these classrooms as the House C teachers use various grouping patterns to provide instruction.

Whole-Class Instruction

Mr. Ruiz is using a variety of grouping methods to teach this interdisciplinary unit on hurricanes with his teaching partners. He begins the unit on natural disasters with a whole-class discussion on storms. Mr. Ruiz uses the KWL strategy and begins class with the question, What do you think you know about storms? The students in House C contribute various ideas, including: they wreck houses, you can't sail during a storm, there are warnings for storms coming, and there are lots of kinds of storms. Mr. Ruiz then asks his students, "What do you want to know about storms?" This question causes a flurry of conversation. The students in House C want to know about the causes of storms, how to detect their arrival, how to prevent them, and what to do during an emergency. Mr. Ruiz then provides the whole class with a journal prompt, providing students with new journals to use for the storm unit and inviting them to make the first entry. "Thinking About Storms" is the title of the first journal entry. Mr. Ruiz ends this whole-class session with a read-aloud of *Eye of the Storm: Chasing Storms with Warren Faidley* (Kramer, 1997).

Learning Stations and Centers

Later during the week, Mr. Ruiz provides his science class with content information about storms using the Center Activity Rotation System (CARS) (Lapp, Flood, & Goss, 2000). Within this rotation system, students are divided into heterogeneous, cooperative groups. Each of the groups works at one of four learning stations designed to build background knowledge, using a four-day rotation. Mr. Ruiz has designed one station to focus on the deadliest hurricane in U.S. history, the Galveston storm of 1906. At this station, he has provided various print and nonprint materials and a list of questions about the Galveston storm. At a second station, Mr. Ruiz has bookmarked an interactive site sponsored by the Discovery Channel on a classroom computer so that students can create their own hurricane by manipulating variables like humidity, water temperature, and wind shear (http://www.discovery.com/stories/science/hurricanes/create.html), and then compare the hurricane they have created with other real hurricanes. A third station includes tracking maps displaying the paths of major storms over the last century. The fourth station features information about evacuation timetables in the coastal areas of the Southeast.

Additionally, Mr. Ruiz daily works at a teacher center with a small, homogeneous group on reading and discussing leveled text passages on hurricanes to provide information through direct, explicit teaching. Mr. Ruiz also meets with individual students as needed. On the fifth day, students work at the center that they missed while they were at the teacher center, and Mr. Ruiz circulates through the groups to gather informal assessment information. Students at each of the learning stations use their journals to record information about the lesson and respond to questions that are raised by the teacher and their peers.

Cooperative Grouping

In Ms. Weiss's social studies class, students in House C work in small cooperative, heterogeneous groups (Antil, Jenkins, Wayne, & Vadasy, 1998; Flood, Lapp, & Wood, 1998; Johnson & Johnson, 1994) to study charts, maps, and graphs for information about four major twentieth-century hurricanes. Many of the students are English-language learners, so oral fluency is always a consideration when designing groups. One of her goals is to have students interact with one another and share information because she believes this supports the development of language fluency. She has found that the use of language brokers during cooperative groups adds a level of support. Each of the students in the cooperative group has an assignment, such as recorder, timekeeper, and facilitator, to complete the day's task of researching hurricanes through history, including Donna, 1960; Camille, 1969; Hugo, 1989; and Andrew, 1992. These heterogeneous groups will later report on their storm to the class.

Ms. Weiss likes the cooperative groups to share what they have learned as a whole class because it provides an accountability piece for each group and contributes to the overall knowledge base. As the small groups work, Ms. Weiss walks around the room, listens in on each group, provides direct instruction, and answers questions in order to ensure that all students receive individualized instruction.

Individuals and Partners

In Mr. Jimenez's English class, students are reading the novel *The Silent Storm* (Garland, 1995). Mr. Jimenez often reads a chapter aloud and then invites students to read the next chapter with a partner. He believes that these partner reading experiences encourage conversations between students and deepen their understanding of the character, plot, and story. He also knows that these partner conversations allow students to "move into the novel" and result in much richer responses to literature.

In addition to the time spent reading, Mr. Jimenez uses partner activities in reviewing the language used in the book. Student teams are assigned an area of expertise and listen as their teacher reads. Some partners listen for unique vocabulary words, while others listen for "golden phrases," clues about the characters, setting descriptions, or historical connections. At the end of the read-aloud or partner reading, each team shares with the whole class the information they gathered. All students keep running logs on each of these categories in their journals.

Small Groups

Our next stop is with Mrs. Chang, a sixth-grade math teacher. Here we see students working on their culminating project, studying a developing storm created by Mr. Ruiz, and utilizing changing charts and graphs of the storm provided by Ms. Weiss. Each group must issue media releases for the public regarding warnings, evacuation notices, and news stories. Small heterogeneous groups of four craft their responses based on the data. While they are doing so, Mrs. Chang meets with individuals to discuss their work. She uses student-teacher conferences to offer small-group instruction to her students. She believes that this individualized attention has resulted in significant gains in student achievement and motivation.

Table 6.1. Daily Activities or Culminating Activities, Literacy Instruction, and Grouping

	K	Grade 2	Grade 5	Grade 7	Grade 9	Grades 10–12
Daily Activities or Culminating Activities	Shared reading	Class retell	Persuasive writing	Written explanations of math concepts	Journal entry to poetry writing	Reciprocal teaching
Literacy Instruction	Introduce key vocabulary words through flashcards and realia. Using a big book, the teacher models reading and students join in when prompted.	Teacher models a "think-aloud." Students share ideas with a partner, then share out to whole class. Students use content area word wall as they retell information.	In pairs, students read a few examples of persuasive writing. Together, the teacher and students construct a paragraph. Students complete the next paragraph. in pairs and the third paragraph independently.	Use word map for new vocabulary in which students must define the word, write a synonym, illustrate, use in a sentence.	Students "power write", and practice generative sentences. After reading poems individually and as a shared reading, students complete RAFTs.	In groups of four, students engage in reciprocal teaching in which each student assumes the role of summarizer, question generator, clarifyer, and predictor. Notes for each role are taken in a journal and roles and journals are shared regularly.
Grouping	Whole group	Whole group and "partner talk"	Whole group and pairs	Whole and small groups	Whole and groups of five	Groups of four students

CONCLUSIONS

Although permanent ability groups may have been the preferred instructional format for teaching in the past, growing evidence and current practices have demonstrated that student needs can be met through flexible grouping structures. Every instructional episode must be carefully considered so that grouping can be planned effectively. We must be careful to match student needs with the most appropriate group experience. The teachers at Kumeyaay Middle School have demonstrated a variety of ways that students can be effectively grouped for instruction.

Take a look at how our six teachers have grouped their students based on the daily/culminating activity and literacy instruction they have provided (see Table 6.1). All teachers have incorporated whole-group teaching to some extent in order to assess prior knowledge, introduce a concept, and/or model strategies. Remember how all grouping configurations can and should be used in K–12 classrooms.

WHAT DO YOU THINK?

1. Think of your classroom. How are the desks arranged? What is the room environment like? How conducive is the space for different grouping styles? What could you do so whole- and small-group interactions are possible and easy to manage?
2. When is it most effective for you to group students homogeneously? Heterogeneously?
3. What would you say to a colleague who believed that whole-group instruction is the only way to teach students?
4. Content-area instruction is typically taught whole group. How would you group students during math, science, social studies, or fine arts?

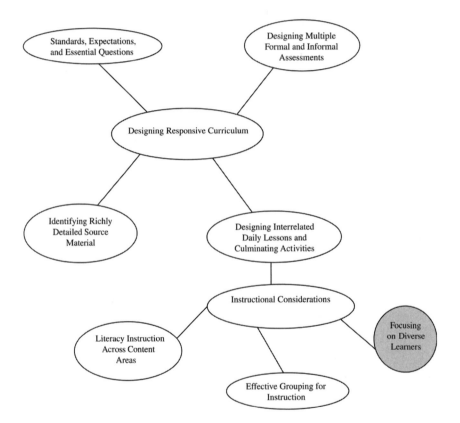

7

FOCUSING ON DIVERSE LEARNERS

The schools of the twenty-first century bustle with promise of the future, a future enriched by the diversity of today's students. An exuberant mix of cultures and languages, abilities, and talents weaves a tapestry of learning in classrooms that maximizes this potential. As with all great possibilities, there is the shadow of failure as well. Schools with diverse student populations, particularly many urban schools, face challenges that mirror the difficulties of the larger society—hunger, neglect, low expectations, even lower self-image, division, and marginalization. Schools have long been viewed as the emergency room of society—a place where the ills of the community are to be bandaged and treated. But triage is not teaching, and treatment is not learning.

The population of a school reflects the community, and its classrooms should as well. The diversity of a school is most often viewed through the three lenses—English-language learners, students identified as gifted or talented, and students with disabilities. These students bring to the classroom their unique talents as well as their support needs. In the past, the prevailing practice was to isolate these learners into discrete groups, in a mistaken belief that a specialized system of supports could then be implemented. However, decades of research have proven that the outcomes do not match the promises. The relationship between ability grouping and pedagogy must be recognized. Nieto (1996) writes,

Students in the lowest levels, for example, are most subjected to rote memorization and worn methods, as their teachers often feel that these are the children who need, first, to master the "basics." Until the basics are learned, the thinking goes, creative methods are a frill that these students can ill afford. Poor children and those most alienated by the schools are once again the losers. The cycle of school failure is repeated: The students most in need are placed in the lowest-level classes and exposed to the drudgery of drill and repetition; school becomes more boring and senseless every day, and the students become discouraged and drop out. (p. 89)

Students identified as gifted have benefited from excellent instruction; the failed promise is in who has been excluded, and in the damage done to a school community when students are separated from their peers. In gifted education, outstanding curriculum design approaches have been developed and implemented, including differentiated instruction (Tomlinson, 1999) and multiple intelligences (Gardner, 1999). But traditional gifted education approaches have failed to overcome the underrepresentation of African Americans (Ford, 1998; Harris & Ford, 1999; Sisk, 1994), Hispanics and Latinos (Strom, 1990), Native Americans (Romero, 1994), English-language learners (Peterson & Margolin, 1997), and students with disabilities (Baum, Olenchak, & Owen, 1998; Hiatt & Covington, 1991); gender imbalance is an issue as well (Sadker, 1999). And most educators are in agreement that these are the students most at risk, and most in need of excellent supports. Doesn't it make sense, then, that well-designed curricular supports are made available to all students, thus circumventing this history of underrepresentation?

School communities suffer when students identified as gifted are singled out for special and often inequitable education. A powerful and destructive message is conveyed to all students when a school endorses the blatant hierarchy of competitive achievement that pits one student against another (Sapon-Shevin, 1994a). As Sapon-Shevin (1994b) notes, separate, "gifted-only" classes disrupt the sense of community on a school campus and serve as a continual reminder of individual worth.

Students with disabilities have also encountered barriers to equity and excellence. Although public schools were designed to provide free and appropriate public education for all students, students identified with disabilities have not always received the same type of education as their peers without disabilities. A continuum of placements was designed to provide a full range of services for individuals with disabilities, from the most restrictive to the least restrictive environments. At one time, a common practice dictated placing individuals with disabilities who required the most intense services in the most restrictive environment, separating them from their same-age peers (U.S. Department of Education, 1999).

Educators now see that separate education often results in social exclusion in school and the community, acquisition of inappropriate behavior, and an inability to generalize knowledge to new environments (Yell, Rogers, & Rogers, 1998). Further, students without disabilities grew up without the experience of knowing peers with disabilities, leaving them ill-prepared to become friends, neighbors, employers, coworkers, parents of individuals with disabilities, or individuals with disabilities themselves (Fisher, Pumpian, & Sax, 1998). Thus, inclusive education has become part of many school reform efforts, affecting not only schools, but also the community (Kennedy & Fisher, 2001).

An inclusive education offers students with disabilities the opportunity to apply functional skills in the general education classroom while also accessing the curriculum standards alongside their peers. Inclusion is typically thought of as the placement of students with disabilities in their neighborhood schools in general education classrooms with peers their own age (NASBE, 1995). Caution must be taken to provide appropriate supports and services in these classrooms for students to be included, versus letting them be "dumped" without support. The coordination of supports and accommodations is necessary for success; indeed, we owe it to all students. The wise practices of inclusive education can serve many students in responsive curriculum classrooms.

In terms of English-language learners, we know that many students who are learning English as a second language do not receive their education in a bilingual classroom or from a bilingual teacher. This may be because of the lack of available personnel, the number of students representing the specific language group, or pressures from politicians and public debate (August & Hakuta, 1998). As a result, many students who are learning English are educated in the "low" group and spend a significant amount of their instructional time with remedial work (Dugan & Desir, 1998). Fortunately, there is a great deal of information available about "sheltered" class instruction for English-language learners in mainstream classes (e.g., Faltis & Wolfe, 1998; Watts-Taffe & Truscott, 2000). While not replacing the need for quality bilingual education, students who are learning English and who are enrolled in content classes require support in order to be successful.

The fields of gifted education, special education, and second-language acquisition offer excellent supports for all learners, not just those identified as possessing a set of characteristics. Compacting, interest groups, and tiered assignments and tests are traditionally gifted practices; Total Physical Response (TPR) and realia are most often associated with second-language acquisition; and accommodations/modifications and scaffolding are usually offered to students with IEPs (Individual Educational Plan). We discuss these practices, as well as writing prompts and concept maps, in this discussion of techniques for supporting all learners in responsive curriculum classrooms. Let's take a tour of some eighth-grade classrooms to see how these strategies are used to support diverse learners.

MIDDLE SCHOOL MEETS THE MIDDLE AGES

The eighth grade at Chavez Middle School (CMS) is waiting for a Renaissance. Not an educational one—that has been happening here for the past decade, as the school has engaged in a whole-school reform effort based on equity and excellence for all its students. Block scheduling began seven years ago, gifted classes were absorbed five years back, and the last of the special education classes was closed three years ago. The school has assembled a track record of success with its innovative approach to supporting diverse learners. The entire school is untracked, meaning that students are not channeled into remedial, average, and honors classes. Instead, all classes are heterogeneously grouped, and individual supports for students identified as gifted (and, for that matter, not identified) are negotiated through independent contracts. Four teachers are assigned to each "house" and 90 students attend classes together. A special educator serves as a support to this house.

The Renaissance that CMS is awaiting is the one that marked an era of tremendous growth in Europe. You see, the eighth grade is in the midst of a two-week interdisciplinary look at the Middle Ages. The unit was designed two years ago through the collaborative efforts of the teachers in the Respeto house. (*Respeto* is the Spanish word for respect; each eighth-grade house has adopted a name that reflects the core values of the school's mission statement.) Ms. Caufield is the science teacher, Mr. Amante teaches English, Mrs. Park is the social studies instructor, and Mr. Tabers teaches mathematics. The house also receives the support of Ms. Duong, the special education teacher. The Respeto teachers named this unit "Middle School Meets the Middle Ages" because they felt it was important for the students to experience what life was like for their peers during that time in history.

Realia

Imagine that you have never seen a castle or a knight in shining armor. How difficult would this lack of experience make your understanding of the Middle Ages? Realia provides learners with an example of the topic or word under study (Lapp, Fisher, & Flood, 1999). Realia can be authentic photos, tangible items, or replications of distinct parts of a larger item. For example, a science teacher often uses a human skeleton to discuss the human bone structure. This same science teacher may use photographs, images, or plastic models of the brain and central nervous system. While reading *What You Never Knew About Fingers, Forks, & Chopsticks* (Lauber, 1999), a teacher may show her second-grade English learners different utensils, from rocks and sticks to grapefruit spoons. Regardless, the realia provided in these lessons builds learners' confidence in their language abilities, makes language learning more relevant, contextualizes the learning, and prepares learners for post-classroom experiences.

In the study of the Middle Ages, Mr. Amante reads aloud the book *Marguerite Makes a Book* (Robertson, 1999). Mr. Amante notices that many of his students have difficulty with several of the ideas presented in this text, including illuminated manuscript, parchment, and quill. To improve their comprehension, Mr. Amante brings samples of each of these items to class for the students to see and touch. In addition, he talks with the art teacher, and together they decide that students should mix colors, make paper, and create their own illuminated manuscripts.

Total Physical Response (TPR)

Total Physical Response is a language development methodology based on the coordination of speech and action developed by James Asher (1996). TPR has been in use for nearly 30 years. While other methods have come and gone, TPR is still a valuable tool when teaching English-language learners (and others for whom language is difficult, such as students with learning disabilities). Despite the wealth of materials available to us, nothing is more useful than this very direct and visual instruction.

With the TPR method, the teacher says a single action word or phrase, such as "stand up" or "put the paper on the table," and then demonstrates the action. At first, students will only be able to follow the command. They may also be able to repeat the teacher's words as they copy the action. The next step is to proceed to more difficult language while still keeping the instruction direct and visual. Many teachers use simple TPR sequences in order to enlarge the students' vocabulary, teach the present continuous and past tense in context, and practice English sentence structure and word order.

When Ms. Caufield uses TPR to provide science lab instructions, she tapes her instructions with background music. This gives her the opportunity to repeat the command, demonstrate the action, and not worry about what command to do next. She can be sure that she has covered all of the actions required of the lab. This tape recorder method also helps her maintain a record of what she has done. Of course, she saves the tapes, shares them with her colleagues, and uses them again with new groups of students.

Scaffolding Instruction

The teachers in the Respeto house all utilize scaffolding to support diverse learners. Scaffolding is the practice of following an instructional sequence to better aid learning. The following is a typical sequence (Wilkinson & Silliman, 2000) the teachers build into their lesson plans:

- Explicit modeling, usually in the form of a demonstration of a strategy or task

- Direct explanations of the strategy or task they have just shared, including the theoretical framework
- Eliciting student response by asking questions and probing for students' construction of meaning
- Verifying and clarifying through further questioning, so that any misinformation can be corrected

This practice echoes Vygotsky's (1978) theory of "zones of proximal development." Vygotsky theorized that when learners receive support just beyond what they can accomplish independently, they learn new skills and concepts.

The teachers of Respeto house have translated this pattern to Show, Tell, Question, and Clarify as a way to utilize scaffolding in the introduction of new material. A lesson in Ms. Caulfield's science class demonstrates this pattern. The class has been studying the spread of diseases in the Middle Ages, some of it due to poor hygiene and medical care. She sets up a lab for students to examine common bacteria using microscopes. She begins by showing the students what they will be doing using a video microscope hooked up to her computer and projected on a screen, thereby allowing all the students to view the prepared slides at 4×, 10×, and 40× powers. She then proceeds to tell them about the three objective lenses of the microscope. Next, she questions students about the advantages and disadvantages of each lens power. Finally, she clarifies some of the misinformation she hears, including Paul's suggestion that the 40× lens would be the best way to locate an object on a slide. She begins the Show, Tell, Question, Clarify sequence again by demonstrating the difficulties of using the 40× lens for that purpose. Ms. Caulfield later comments that showing students first seems to be more useful because students are able to ask higher order questions and many of the procedural details have been demonstrated already.

Compacting

In compacting, students are assessed on their prior knowledge. Those students who already know the material are assigned other tasks, such as peer tutoring, library research, and math labs. This allows Mrs. Park, the social studies teacher, to focus her lesson on the students who really need it. Two rules guide her use of this strategy. First, the pre-assessment changes every week. One week it may be paper-pencil, the next could be small group, the next could be oral, and the following could include a performance. Second, all students must take the final assessment of the material, and their grade is based on that score.

One student, Julian, has "compacted out" because of his level of knowledge about medieval life. However, he had negotiated a contract to receive honors credit in this course. He speaks with Mrs. Park about his interest in the Middle Ages, and proposes translating his peers' projects into a website. He makes an especially compelling case for doing so by comparing it to the role of the monks of the Middle Ages who created the beautiful illuminated manuscripts of the time.

Mrs. Park likes to offer compacting to her students because it has served two purposes. In addition to creating an in-class tutoring system, she has noticed that some of the students who were eligible for "compacting out" decided not to because they learned they did better on the tests when they participated in the lesson. Mrs. Park has found this to be an effective way to engage some of her students.

Independent Projects

Mr. Amante, the English teacher, believes that work done outside of school should be interesting and should require students to work with at least one other person. He is most interested in independent projects (previously called homework) that require students to interact with their families. He is least interested in independent projects that encourage students to sit in their bedroom by themselves. Mr. Amante also likes independent projects that are challenging for students but not frustrating. This has led him to develop several projects, and not have all his students do the same project each night.

For this unit on the Middle Ages, some students interview their elder family members on how the role of children has changed during their lifetime. The unit has focused on the fact that children were not viewed as "children" in modern terms, but rather as little adults. They read informational texts about marriage laws of the time and are shocked to find out that girls married at twelve, and boys at fourteen! They compare their older family members' memories with those of the children of the Middle Ages. Mr. Amante finds this independent project to be particularly successful for the ELL (English-language learners) students because they can complete their assignment in their home language.

Other students work together outside of school to film an I-Movie using the school's digital camera. (I-Movie software allows students to easily film and edit, and then add special effects and titles.) Inspired by their readings of *Catherine, Called Birdy* (Cushman, 1995) and *Matilda Bone* (Cushman, 2000), they create a "day in the life" comparison of a servant girl and the daughter of a lord. Jen, a student with a significant disability, use her Delta Talker augmentative communication device to perform her lines in the docudrama. Ms. Duong, the special education teacher, programmed the device in advance for Jen and her friends. Julian has plans to include this short I-Movie on the website.

Interest Groups

Chavez Middle School has an advisory period so that only half the students are at lunch at one time. The half who are not at lunch sign up for an advisory class based on the topics covered. For example, Ms. Duong, the special educator, has offered topics as diverse as the *Titanic*, 3-D art, horror novels, and careers in human services. These advisories are full of students interested in a specific topic and last for three weeks. At the end of the three weeks, students get to pick a new topic. Some students pick Ms. Duong regardless of what she is doing; others make different choices each term. Ms. Duong believes that these interest groups allow students to experience the richness of a curriculum and make choices about what they want to learn. She knows that the time she spends in advisory allows her to get to know students very well.

Concept Maps and Character Webs

Visual representations of complex ideas help students organize information. Developing concept or semantic maps is one strategy used by teachers because it provides insights about students' knowledge about the topic. Typically, the main idea is placed in the center of the paper with a small circle drawn around it. Then lines are drawn from the circle to ideas that connect with the main idea. As you can imagine, there can be several subideas to a main idea, and each subidea can have branches of ideas from it.

For example, Ms. Caulfield's science class is studying the plague, also known as the Black Death because of the black splotches on the victim's skin. They have examined the probable path of the disease, from its origins in Asia Minor around 1346 to its spread by *rattus rattus*, the common ship rat, along the major trade routes between East and West. They have studied population charts and copies of primary source materials, such as census reports, and have discovered that an estimated 25 million people died in the five years between 1347 and 1352. They have charted hygiene habits of the time (many people completely bathed only once, on their wedding day), food storage (salt was the major means of preserving meat), and medical treatments such as leeches and dunkings. One day Ms. Caulfield asks each student to take out a piece of paper and write inside a small circle the words *Black Death*. The students are then asked to brainstorm lots of ideas that are connected to their main idea. Following this brainstorming, students are asked to transform their concept map into a three-paragraph paper. Ms. Caulfield's students will expand these concept maps again near the end of the unit, done in groups of four, as a way to review for the test. Not only can her students review information this way, but she can also gain insights about areas that students may not understand.

Mr. Amante uses character webs to focus his students' thinking on people during his English class. He reads aloud the chapter book *The Door in the Wall* (De Angeli, 1990), a story about a young English boy who acquires a disability and is abandoned by the superstitious servants who were charged with caring for him. Each student is given a simple drawing of a person's head. As they learned more about Robin (the main character in the book), the students illustrate the simple drawing and place key words around the head to describe him. Mr. Amante has found that the character webs help all of his students understand character development. He was especially pleased to find that students identified as having learning disabilities significantly improved their understanding of the story when they were required to create character webs. In addition to concept maps, Mr. Amante also uses clip art, illustrated vocabulary, videos, and computer websites to assist students in creating visual representations.

Writing Prompts and Questions

Mrs. Park works with students to create a series of questions to answer as they read the social studies textbook and informational text. She has found that this helps focus their reading for specific information. This may be as simple as having students read the end-of-chapter questions prior to and throughout the reading of the chapter. (Many of the students thought this was "cheating" when she first suggested it! She assured them that it's what effective readers do.) Focusing on the questions helps students chunk, summarize, and synthesize the newly acquired information. When there are no end-of-unit questions, Mrs. Park and her students create questions that focus their reading. These questions are often first developed during the "what I want to learn" part of the KWL (Ogle, 1986) or by changing text subheadings into questions.

Students are divided into expert groups of six to read *How Would You Survive the Middle Ages?* (MacDonald, 1997), *Keeping Clean: Everyday History* (Stewart, 2000), *Life During the Middle Ages: The Way People Live* (Rice, 2000), or *Eyewitness: Medieval Life* (Langley, Dann, & Brightling, 2000). They search for answers to the questions generated during the KWL, and then convert the questions and answers into a Trivial Pursuit game. As a culminating project, all the cards from the classes are combined for use in Ye Olde Medieval Trivial Pursuit Tournament. Their performance on the end-of-unit test suggests to Mrs. Park that generating questions and answers is an effective study tool for her students.

During writing assignments, Mrs. Park has found that students perform better when she changes the questions into sentence starters. For example, instead of asking students to respond to a question like, "What is the role of a vassal?" she rephrases it to read, "The role of a vassal is to . . ." Additional examples she has developed include: "The economic effect of the Black Death was . . ." and "The Moors influence on European learning included . . ." This format for questioning is especially effective for her English-language learners, who sometimes struggle with interrogatives in a new language, as well as her students with learning disabilities.

Ms. Duong, the special education teacher, also provides clip art cutouts for Sonia and Tre, two students with significant disabilities, so that they can choose appropriate art to augment their dictated responses.

Tiered Assignments and Tests

Mr. Tabers, the mathematics teacher, has found that when students have choice in their assignments, they perform better. For this reason, he has a full page of assignments that students can do for his class. Each assignment is worth a maximum number of points, and students select which assignments to complete based on their interests. While other teachers have different rules regarding tiered assignments, Mr. Tabers lets his students do as many assignments as they want in order to earn the grade that they want in his class. For the Middle Schools Meets the Middle Ages unit, students can select a variety of medieval card games to research, construct, and then teach the class. These games include Piquet, a card game that relies on mental math; Noddy, an early version of cribbage that creates number sequences; or Byzantine chess, a tenth-century precursor of the modern game, played on a round board. Byzantine chess represents a more difficult mathematical challenge because students who choose this game must work in three-dimensional space.

In addition to the tiered assignments, Mr. Tabers uses tiered tests. His end-of-unit tests have five parts: true/false, multiple choice, short answer, short essay with illustration, and long essay. Mr. Tabers likes for his students to have experiences with different ways of demonstrating their knowledge so that they will do well on the statewide assessments. His use of tiered tests is unique. During test time, students are required to complete two sections of the test. When he returns the test the following day, he has graded the two sections that each student completed. The students then complete one more section of the test. He does this for several reasons. First, students can demonstrate their knowledge the best way they know how. Second, students learn to use the test as a tool. That is, there are answers to questions in other questions on a test. Third, students talk about the test during passing periods and lunch after the first administration. While the students think they are being sly, Mr. Tabers likes the fact that they are using their time to talk about the curriculum. Finally, he likes the idea that these tests communicate to students that knowledge is never complete, that there is always more to know and learn.

Accommodations and Modifications

Accommodations and modifications are techniques used by special educators to ensure that students with disabilities can access the core curriculum in general education classrooms (e.g., Castagnera, Fisher, Rodifer, & Sax, 1998). An accommodation is a change made to the teaching or testing procedures in order to provide a student with access to information and to create an equal opportunity to demonstrate knowledge and skills. Accommodations do not change the instructional level, content, or performance criteria for meeting the standards. Examples of accommodations include enlarging the print, Braille versions, providing oral versions of tests, and using calculators.

A modification is a change in what a student is expected to learn and/or demonstrate. While a student may be working on modified course content, the subject area remains the same as the rest of the class. If the decision is made to modify the curriculum, it is done in a variety of ways, for a variety of reasons, with a variety of outcomes. Again, modifications vary according to the situation. Listed below are four modification techniques:

- Same—Only Less. The assignment remains the same except the number of items are reduced. The items selected should be representative of the curriculum. For example, a social studies test that consists of multiple choice questions, each with five possible answers, can be modified and the number of possible answers reduced to two.
- Streamline the Curriculum. The assignment is reduced in size, breadth, or focus to emphasize the key points. For example, in a language arts class, students may create an author study on Gary Paulsen with a reflective journal on themes and impressions of the books they read. A student with a disability may focus on identifying the themes of the books he or she reads, and then create a display that uses pictures to support his or her writing on those main ideas.

- Same Activity with Infused Objective. The assignment remains the same but additional components such as IEP objectives or skills identified are incorporated. This is often done in conjunction with other accommodations and/or modifications to ensure that all IEP objectives are addressed. For example, if a student has an IEP objective to answer factual and inferential questions, the math teacher may need to remember to ask these types of questions so that the student can practice this skill in a natural setting.
- Curriculum Overlapping. The assignment in one area may be completed during another time. Some students work slowly and need more time to complete assignments, while others need to explore the connections between various content areas. This strategy is especially helpful in these situations. For example, if a student participates in a poster project in his or her cooperative learning group during math centers, the product can also be used during language arts.

Deciding which technique to use depends on the type of assignment and the specific student. One assignment may only need to be reduced in size in order for the student to be successful, while another may incorporate infused objectives. Each of the techniques, as well as appropriate personal supports, should be considered for each situation. Keep in mind that curriculum does not always need to be modified—even when considering students with significant disabilities. When general education teachers provide multilevel instruction, changes to a lesson may not be necessary. Differentiating instruction allows all students a variety of ways to demonstrate knowledge while continuing to meet the requirements of the class. At other times, the curriculum can be made more accessible through accommodations and modifications.

CONCLUSION

As you can tell, many of the supports that diverse learners require can be provided as part of the instructional arrangements in the general education classroom. Several years of research suggests that these instructional strategies are beneficial for all students, not only those identified as gifted, English-language learners, or those with disabilities. Taken together, curriculum and instructional supports address many of the support needs for diverse learners.

Let's take one last look at our six teachers to see how they have focused on their diverse learners during a specific daily or culminating activity (see Table 7.1). Notice how many of the ideas for teaching diverse students can be applied from kindergarten through high school.

While reading from a big book, Mr. G uses flashcards with picture supports to reinforce key vocabulary words to his kindergarten students. In addition, realia is used to further allow the students to touch and manipulate objects that appear in the text. Mr. G is especially good at questioning his students based on their strengths and needs of a literacy learner. Students who are new to the country are given the opportunity to point to pictures, use hand motions, and explain their thinking in their native language in order to feel like a contributing member of the class.

Ms. Pham-Barron's diverse class is used to being "buddied" up with students who have different and complementary skills. The students also role-play some of the historical events they read about to make the content come to life. Some students need to listen to the text a second or third time using headphones at the listening post before writing their retell.

Ms. Allen provides her students with different examples of persuasive writing at their reading level. While questioning her fifth-grade students, Ms. Allen differentiates the questions she asks depending on their language and literacy proficiencies. As she models the first paragraph of a persuasive essay, she uses different colored overhead markers to highlight important components and key phrases.

Ms. Mellander has many resources available to help support the diverse learners in her classroom. Her print-rich environment includes math word walls, reference charts, calculator posters, and texts at varying levels. Students are encouraged to use calculators and fraction strips as they explain how decimals are converted into percentages. Some students are allowed to orally respond to the assignment using a tape recorder.

Mr. Hernandez creates a very comfortable environment for his ninth-grade diverse learners as students chorally read the poem. The text is displayed on the overhead projector and also given to students so they can underline key phrases and words for themselves using highlighters. Mr. Hernandez shows his students magazine articles, photos, and video clips of the 9/11 disaster in order stimulate ideas and tap into their prior knowledge.

While Ms. Grant's high school students work in reciprocal teaching groups, some students with special needs are encouraged to organize their thoughts into pictures rather than words. Starter sentences are also provided for students who need to refer to a modeled prompt. Because Ms. Grant believes that students grasp new concepts when readings and conversations relate to real life situations, she brings in pertinent handouts, articles, and examples from film clips to engage her learners.

WHAT DO YOU THINK?

1. What is the range of literacy that exists in your classroom?
2. Think of your instructional materials. If a student new to the country became a member of your classroom community tomorrow, which of these materials would help support this English-language learner? Think of this same scenario as if a student with a disability entered your room.
3. What are some strategies you use to differentiate instruction to meet the needs of all students?

Table 7.1. Daily Activities or Culminating Activities, Literacy Instruction, Grouping, and Focusing on Diverse Learners

	K	Grade 2	Grade 5	Grade 7	Grade 9	Grades 10–12
Daily Activities or Culminating Activities	Shared reading	Class retell	Persuasive writing	Written explanations of math concepts	Journal entry to poetry writing	Reciprocal teaching
Literacy Instruction	Introduce key vocabulary words through flashcards and realia. Using a big book, the teacher models reading and students join in when prompted.	Teacher models a "think-aloud." Students share ideas with a partner, then share out to whole class. Students use content area word wall as they retell information.	In pairs, students read a few examples of persuasive writing. Together, the teacher and students construct a paragraph. Students complete the next paragraph in pairs and the third paragraph independently.	Use word map for new vocabulary in which students must define the word, write a synonym, illustrate, use in a sentence.	Students "power write" and practice generative sentences. After reading poems individually and as a shared reading, students complete RAFTs.	In groups of four, students engage in reciprocal teaching in which each student assumes the role of summarizer, question generator, clarifyer, and predictor. Notes for each role are taken in a journal and roles and journals are shared regularly.

(continued)

Table 7.1. (continued)

	K	Grade 2	Grade 5	Grade 7	Grade 9	Grades 10–12
Grouping	Whole group	Whole group and "partner talk"	Whole group and pairs	Whole and small groups	Whole and groups of five	Groups of four students
Focusing on Diverse Learners	Use flashcards with supporting pictures, realia, different levels of questioning	Role-play historical events, pair students with different and complementary skills, allow students to listen to text using headphones at a listening center	Provide examples of persuasive writing written at different levels, differentiate levels of questioning, use different color code and underline important words and phrases	Use graphing calculator, post reference charts, provide fractions strips as manipulatives, allow oral responses using a tape recorder	Choral read poem, encourage oral contributions rather than written, provide visual aids to stimulate interest, color code and underline important words and phrases	Pair students with different and complementary skills, provide sample sentences for students to use as a model, relate problems to real-life situations

REFERENCES

REFERENCES

Alexander, P. A., & Jetton, T. L. (2000). Learning from text: A multidimensional and developmental perspective. In M. L. Kamil, P. B. Mosenthal, P. D. Pearson, & R. Barr (Eds.), *Handbook of reading research: Vol. 3* (pp. 285–310). Mahwah, NJ: Lawrence Erlbaum.

Allen, J., & Gonzalez, K. (1998). *There's room for me here: Literacy workshop in the middle school.* York, ME: Stenhouse.

Allor, J. H. (2003). Developing emergent literacy skills through storybook reading. *Intervention in School and Clinic, 39,* 72–79.

Almasi, J. F. (1995). The nature of fourth graders' sociocognitive conflicts in peer-led and teacher-led discussions of literature. *Reading Research Quarterly, 30,* 314–351.

Alvermann, D. E. (1991). The discussion web: A graphic aid for learning across the curriculum. *The Reading Teacher, 45,* 92–99.

Alvermann, D. E., & Hagood, M. C. (2000). Fandom and critical media literacy. *Journal of Adolescent & Adult Literacy, 43,* 436–446.

Amer, A. A. (1997). The effect of the teacher's reading aloud on the reading comprehension of ESL students. *ELT Journal 1997, 51*(1), 43–47.

Ames, R., & Ames, C. (Eds.). (1984). *Research on motivation in education: Vol. 1. Student motivation.* New York: Academic Press.

Anders, P. L., & Bos, C. S. (1986). Semantic feature analysis: An interactive strategy for vocabulary development and text comprehension. *Journal of Reading, 29,* 610–616.

Andrews, S. E. (1997). Writing to learn in content area reading class. *Journal of Adolescent & Adult Literacy, 41,* 141–142.

Antil, L. R., Jenkins, J. R., Wayne, S. K., & Vadasy, P. F. (1998). Cooperative learning: Prevalence, conceptualizations, and the relation between research and practice. *American Educational Research Journal, 35,* 419–454.

Aronson, E. (2000). *Nobody left to hate: Teaching compassion after Columbine.* New York: A. Worth.

Asher, J. J. (1996). *Learning another language through actions* (5th ed.). Los Gatos, CA: Sky Oaks Productions.

Atkins, B. (1994). Diversity: A continuing rehabilitation challenge and opportunity. In S. Walker, K. A. Turner, M. Haile-Michael, A. Vincent, & M. D. Miles (Eds.), *Disability and diversity: New leadership for a new era.* Washington, DC: Howard University.

Atwell, N. (1998). *In the middle: New understandings about writing, reading, and learning* (2nd ed.). Portsmouth, NH: Boynton/Cook.

August, D., & Hakuta, K. (Eds.). (1998). *Educating language-minority children.* Washington, DC: National Academy Press.

Ausubel, D. P. (1978). In defense of advance organizers: A reply to the critics. *Review of Educational Research, 48,* 251–257.

Banks, J. A. (1973). *Teaching strategies for social studies.* Reading, MA: Addison-Wesley.

Barton, M. L. (1997). Addressing the literacy crisis: Teaching reading in the content areas. *NASSP Bulletin, 81*(587), 22–30.

Baum, S. M., Olenchak, F. R., & Owen, S. V. (1998). Gifted students with attention deficits: Fact and/or fiction? Or, can we see the forest for the trees? *Gifted Child Quarterly, 42*(2), 96–104.

Baumann, J. F. (1986). Effect of rewritten content textbook passages on middle grade students' comprehension of main ideas: Making the inconsiderate considerate. *Journal of Reading Behavior, 18*(1), 1–21.

Bear, D. R., Templeton, S., Invernizzi, M., & Johnson, F. (1996). *Words their way: Word study for phonics, vocabulary, and spelling instruction.* Upper Saddle River, NJ: Prentice Hall.

Beck, C., Gilles, C., O'Connor, A., & Koblitz, D. (1999). The Midwest: Life in the Mississippi River Valley. *Language Arts, 76,* 525–532.

Beck, I. L., McKeown, M. G., Hamilton, R. L., & Kucan, L. (1997). *Questioning the author: An approach for enhancing student engagement with text.* Newark, DE: International Reading Association.

Beck, I. L., McKeown, M. G., Worthy, J., Sandora, C. A., & Kucan, L. L. (1993). *Questioning the author: A year-long classroom implementation to engage students with text* (Technical Report). Pittsburgh: University of Pittsburgh, Learning Research and Development Center.

Beerens, D. R. (2000). *Evaluating teachers for professional growth: Creating a culture of motivation and learning.* Thousand Oaks, CA: Corwin.

Brandt, R. (2003). Will the real standards-based education please stand up? *Leadership, 32,* 17–21.

Bruner, J. (1966). *Toward a theory of instruction.* Cambridge, MA: Harvard University Press.

Bryant, D. P., Ugel, N., Hamff, A., & Thompson, S. (1999). Instructional strategies for content-area reading instruction. *Intervention in School and Clinic, 34,* 293–302.

Calfee, R. C., & Gearhart, M. (1998). Introduction: Portfolios and large-scale assessment. *Educational Assessment, 5,* 1–3.

Calfee, R. C., & Hiebert, E. H. (1991). Classroom assessment in reading. In R. Barr, M. Kamil, P. Rosenthal, & P. D. Pearson (Eds.), *Handbook of research on reading* (2nd ed., pp. 281–309). New York: Longman.

Calkins, L. M. (1986). *The art of teaching writing.* Portsmouth, NH: Heinemann.

Carr, R. (1997). Writing a soundtrack to your life. *General Music Today, 11*(1), 21–23.

Cassady, J. K. (1998). Wordless books: No-risk tools for inclusive middle-grade classrooms. *Journal of Adolescent & Adult Literacy, 41,* 428–433.

Castagnera, E., Fisher, D., Rodifer, K., & Sax, C. (1998). *Deciding what to teach and how to teach it: Connecting students through curriculum and instruction.* Colorado Springs, CO: PEAK Parent Center.

Cazden, C. B. (1986). Classroom discourse. In M. C. Wittrock (Ed.), *Handbook of research on teaching* (3rd ed., pp. 432–463). New York: Macmillan.

Chen, J., Krechevsky, M., Viens, J., & Isberg, E. (1998). *Project Zero frameworks for early childhood education: Vol. 1. Building on children's strengths: The experience of Project Spectrum.* New York: Teachers College Press.

Christ, G. M. (1995). Curriculums with real-world connections. *Educational Leadership, 52*(8), 32–35.

Chudowsky, N. (2003). Large-scale assessments that support learning: What will it take? *Theory into Practice, 42,* 75–83.

Ciborowski, J. (1992). *Textbooks and the students who can't read them.* Cambridge, MA: Brookline.

Clay, M. (1985). *The early detection of reading difficulties* (3rd ed.). Portsmouth, NH: Heinemann.

Cohen, E. (1986). *Designing groupwork: Strategies for the heterogeneous classroom*. New York: Teachers College Press.

Cohen, E. (1994). Restructuring the classroom: Conditions for productive small groups. *Review of Educational Research, 64,* 1–35.

Combs, M., & Beach, J. D. (1994). Stories and storytelling: Personalizing the social studies. *The Reading Teacher, 47,* 464–471.

Copley, J. (2003). Assessing mathematical learning: Observing and listening to children. *Child Care Information Exchange, 151,* 47–50.

Courtney, A. M., & Abodeeb, T. L. (1999). Diagnostic-reflective portfolios. *The Reading Teacher, 52,* 708–714.

Covey, S. B. (1990). *The 7 habits of highly effective people: Powerful lessons in personal change*. New York: Fireside.

Cunningham, P. M., Hall, D. P., & Defee, M. (1998). Nonability-grouped, multilevel instruction: Eight years later. *The Reading Teacher, 51,* 652–664.

Custer, R. L. (1995). Rubrics: An authentic assessment tool for technology education. *Technology Teacher, 55*(4), 27–37.

Dahl, K. L., & Farnan, N. (1998). *Children's writing: Perspectives from research*. Newark, DE: International Reading Association and National Reading Conference.

Daniels, H., & Zemelman, S. (2003). Out with textbooks, in with learning. *Educational Leadership, 61*(4), 36–40.

DeVries, D., & Edwards, K. (1974). Student teams and learning groups. Their effects on cross-race and cross-sex interaction. *Journal of Educational Psychology, 66,* 741–749.

Dewey, J. (1998). Experience, knowledge, and value: A rejoinder. In J. A. Boydston (Ed.), *John Dewey: The later works, 1925–1953* (Vol. 15, pp. 3–90). Carbondale: Southern University Press (Original work published 1939).

Diamond, M., & Hopson, J. (1998). *Magic trees of the mind: How to nurture your child's intelligence, creativity and healthy emotions from birth through adolescence*. New York: Dutton.

Doyle, W. (1996). Curriculum and pedagogy. In P. W. Jackson (Ed.), *Handbook of research on curriculum* (pp. 486–516). New York: Macmillan.

Dreeben, R., & Barr, R. (1988). The formation and instruction of ability groups. *American Journal of Education, 97,* 34–64.

Dreher, M. J. (1998–1999). Motivating children to read more nonfiction. *The Reading Teacher, 52,* 414–417.

Dugan, S., & Desir, L. (1998). Ethnography and "Lucy": ESL students in the "content" class. *Research and Teaching in Developmental Education, 14*(2), 51–57.

Espinosa, R., & Ochoa, A. (1992, Spring). *The educational attainment of California youth: A public equity crisis.* San Diego, CA: Multifunctional Resource Center.

Evans, R. W. (1997). Teaching social issues: Implementing an issues-centered curriculum. In E.W. Ross (Ed.), *The social studies curriculum: Purposes, problems, and possibilities* (pp. 197–212). Albany, NY: SUNY.

Faltis, C. J., & Wolfe, P. M. (Eds.). (1998). *So much to say: Adolescents, bilingualism, and ESL in the secondary school.* New York: Teachers College.

Farnan, N. (1996). Connecting adolescents and reading: Goals at the middle level. *Journal of Adolescent & Adult Literacy, 39,* 436–445.

Fields, M. V., & Spangler, K. L. (1995). Let's begin reading right: Developmentally appropriate beginning literacy (3rd ed.). Englewood Cliffs, NJ: Prentice Hall.

Fisher, D., Pumpian, I., & Sax, C. (1998). High school students' attitudes about and recommendations for their peers with significant disabilities. *Journal of the Association for Persons with Severe Handicaps, 23,* 272–282.

Fisher, D., Sax, C., & Pumpian, I. (Eds.). (1999). *Inclusive high schools: Learning from contemporary classrooms.* Baltimore, MD: Paul H. Brookes.

Fitzgerald, M. A., & Byers, A. (2002). A rubric for selecting inquiry-based activities. *Science Scope, 26,* 22–25.

Flood, J., & Lapp, D. (1995). Broadening the lens: Toward an expanded conceptualization of literacy. In K. A. Hinchman, D. J. Leu, & C. K. Kinzer (Eds.), *The Forty-fourth Yearbook of the National Reading Conference* (pp. 1–16). Chicago: NRC.

Flood, J., Lapp, D., Flood, S., & Nagel, G. (1992). Am I allowed to group? Using flexible patterns for effective instruction. *The Reading Teacher, 44,* 608–616.

Flood, J., Lapp, D., & Wood, K. (1997). *Staff development guide.* New York: Macmillan/McGraw-Hill.

Flood, J., Lapp, D., & Wood, K. (1998). Viewing: The neglected communication process or "when what you see isn't what you get." *The Reading Teacher, 52,* 300–304.

Ford, D. Y. (1998). The underrepresentation of minority students in gifted education: Problems and promises in recruitment and retention. *Journal of Special Education, 32,* 4–14.

Freedman, R. A. (1995). The Mr. and Mrs. club: The value of collaboration in writers' workshop. *Language Arts, 72,* 97–104.

Freese, A. R. (1999). The role of reflection on preservice teachers' development in the context of a professional development school. *Teaching and Teacher Education, 15,* 895–909.

Frey, J. (1998). *Maximizing reader response through films and videos*. Unpublished master's thesis, San Diego State University, San Diego, CA.

Frey, N., & Hiebert, E. H. (2003). Teacher-based assessment of literacy learning. In J. Flood, D. Lapp, J. R. Squire, & J. M. Jensen (Eds.), *Handbook of research on teaching the English language arts* (2nd ed., pp. 608–618). Mahwah, NJ: Lawrence Erlbaum.

Friant, D. (2002). Please pass the cheesecake and curriculum guides: Meeting the principle of collaborative planning. *Teacher Librarian, 30*, 63.

Fry, E. B. (1969). The readability graph validated at primary levels. *The Reading Teacher, 22*, 534–538.

Gamoran, A. (1989). Measuring curriculum differentiation. *American Journal of Education, 97*, 129–143.

Ganske, K., Monroe, J. K., & Strickland, D. (2003). Questions teachers ask about struggling readers and writers. *The Reading Teacher, 57*, 118–128.

Gardner, H. (1999). *Intelligence reframed: Multiple intelligences for the 21st century*. New York: Basic Books.

Garry, A., et. al. (2003). Advice from the experts. *Technology & Learning, 23*, 28–30.

Glasswell, K., Parr, J., & McNaughton, S. (2003). Four ways to work against yourself when conferencing with struggling writers. *Language Arts, 80*, 291–298.

Goerss, B. L. (1998). Incorporating picture books into content classrooms. *Indiana Reading Journal, 30*(3), 30–35.

Goldman, S. R., & Rakestraw, J. A., Jr. (2000). Structural aspects of constructing meaning from text. In M. L. Kamil, P. B. Mosenthal, P. D. Pearson, & R. Barr (Eds.) *Handbook of reading research: Vol. 3* (pp. 311–335). Mahwah, NJ: Lawrence Erlbaum.

Goodman, Y. (1985). Kidwatching: Observing children in the classroom. In A. Jaggar & M. T. Smith-Burke (Eds.), *Observing the language learner* (pp. 9–18). Newark, DE: International Reading Association.

Graves, D. (1983). *Writing: Teachers and children at work*. Exeter, NH: Heinemann.

Green, J. L., Harker, J. O., & Golden, J. M. (1987). Lesson construction: Differing views. In G. W. Nobblitt & W. T. Pink (Eds.), *Schooling in social context: Qualitative studies* (pp. 46–77). Norwood, NJ: Ablex.

Haberman, M. (2000). Urban schools: Day camp or custodial centers? *Phi Delta Kappan, 82*, 203–208.

Haller, E. (1985). Pupil race and elementary school reading grouping: Are teachers biased against black children? *American Educational Research Journal, 22*, 409–418.

Haller, E., & Davis, S. (1980). Does socioeconomic status bias the assignment of elementary school students to reading groups? *American Educational Research Journal, 17*, 772–781.

Harp, B. (1994). *Assessment and evaluation for student-centered learning.* Norwood, MA: Christopher-Gordon.

Harris, J. J., III., & Ford, D. Y. (1999). Hope deferred again: Minority students underrepresented in gifted programs. *Education and Urban Society, 31*, 225–237.

Henkin, R. (1995). Insiders and outsiders in first-grade writing workshops: Gender and equity issues. *Language Arts, 72*, 429–434.

Hermann, B. A. (1998). Two approaches for helping poor readers become more strategic. In R. L. Allington (Ed.), *Teaching struggling readers* (pp. 168–174). Newark, DE: International Reading Association.

Heuwinkel, M. (1996). New ways of learning = New ways of teaching. *Childhood Education, 73*, 27.

Hiatt, E. L., & Covington, J. (1991). Identifying and serving diverse populations. (ERIC Clearinghouse ED 340 164)

Hiebert, E. (1983). An examination of ability grouping for reading instruction. *Reading Research Quarterly, 18*, 231–255.

Howard, T. C. (2003). Who receives the short end of the shortage? Implications of the U.S. teacher shortage on urban schools. *Journal of Curriculum and Supervision, 18*, 142–160.

Huffman, E. S. (1998). Authentic rubrics. *Art Education, 51*, 64–68.

Hunter, M. C. (1994). *Enhancing teaching.* New York: Macmillan.

Indrisano, R., & Paratore, J. R. (1991). Classroom contexts for literacy learning. In J. Flood, J. M. Jensen, D. Lapp, & J. R. Squire (Eds.), *Handbook of research on teaching the English language arts* (pp. 477–488). New York: Macmillan.

Irvin, J. L., Lunstrum, J. P., Lynch-Brown, C., & Shepard, M. F. (1995). *Enhancing social studies through literacy strategies.* Bulletin 91. Washington, DC: National Council for the Social Studies.

Johnson, D. W., & Johnson, R. T. (1994). *Learning together and alone: Cooperative, competitive, and individualistic learning* (4th ed.). Boston: Allyn & Bacon.

Johnson, D. W., Johnson, R. T., & Maruyama, G. (1983). Interdependence and interpersonal attraction among heterogeneous and homogeneous individuals: A theoretical formulation and meta-analysis of research. *Review of Educational Research, 53*, 5–54.

Johnson, N. M., & Ebert, M. J. (1992). Time travel is possible: Historical fiction and biography—Passport to the past. *The Reading Teacher, 45*, 488–495.

Johnston, P. H., & Winograd, P. N. (1985). Passive failure in reading. *Journal of Reading Behavior, 17,* 279–301.

Jorgensen, C. M. (1994). Essential questions—Inclusive answers. *Educational Leadership, 52*(4), 52–55.

Kennedy, C. H., & Fisher, D. (2001). *Inclusive middle schools.* Baltimore, MD: Paul H. Brookes.

Koretz, S. (1999). *A study of fourth grade students' reading and thinking behaviors during social studies class when using multiple sources strategies.* Unpublished master's thesis, San Diego State University, San Diego, CA.

Kuhn, D. (1999). A developmental model of critical thinking. *Educational Researcher, 28*(2), 16–26.

Lapp, D., Fisher, D., & Flood, J. (1999). Integrating the language arts and content areas: Effective research-based strategies. *The California Reader, 32*(4), 35–38.

Lapp, D., Fisher, D., Flood, J., & Cabello, A. (2000). An integrated approach to the teaching and assessment of language arts. In S. Hurley & J. Tinajero (Eds.), *Assessing literacy for English language learners* (pp. 1–26). Boston: Allyn & Bacon.

Lapp, D., Fisher, D., Flood, J., Geiss, R., & Flood, S. (1999). *Effective classroom grouping* (videotape). California Department of Education & San Diego State University, School of Teacher Education. Retrieved from http://coe.sdsu.edu/readingvideos/

Lapp, D., & Flood, J. (1992). *Teaching reading to every child* (3rd ed.). New York: Macmillan.

Lapp, D., Flood, J., & Farnan, N. (1996). *Content area reading and learning: Instructional strategies* (2nd ed.). Needham Heights, MA: Simon & Schuster.

Lapp, D., Flood, J., & Fisher, D. (1999). Intermediality: How the use of multiple media enhances learning. *The Reading Teacher, 52,* 776–780.

Lapp, D., Flood, J., & Goss, K. (2000). Desks don't move—students do: In effective classroom environments. *The Reading Teacher, 54,* 31–36.

Lapp, D., Flood, J., & Hoffman, R. (1996). Using concept mapping as an effective strategy in content area instruction. In D. Lapp, J. Flood, & N. Farnan (Eds.), *Content area reading and learning: Instructional strategies* (pp. 291–306). Boston: Allyn & Bacon.

Lapp, D., Flood, J., & Ranck-Buhr, W. (1997). Flexible theme-based centers: Methods and operations. In J. Flood, D. Lapp, & K. D. Wood (Eds.), *Staff development guide for middle school teachers* (pp. 239–244). New York: Macmillan.

Lee, V. E., & Burkam, D. T. (2003). Dropping out of high school: The role of school organization and structure. *American Educational Research Journal, 40,* 353–393.

Leitze, A. R., & Mau, S. T. (1999). Assessing problem-solving thought. *Mathematics Teaching in the Middle School, 4,* 305–311.

Lemke, J. L. (1990). *Talking science.* Norwood, NJ: Ablex.

Leslie, L., & Jett-Simpson, M. (1997). *Authentic literacy assessment: An ecological approach.* New York: Longman.

Lipton, L., & Hubble, D. (1997). *More than 50 ways to learner-centered literacy.* Arlington Heights, IL: IRI/Skylight Training and Publishing.

Lobach, M. R. (1995). Kids explore heritage through writer's workshop and professional publication. *The Reading Teacher, 48,* 522–524.

Macdonald, J. B., & Purpel, D. E. (1987). Curriculum and planning: Visions and metaphors. *Journal of Curriculum and Supervision, 2,* 178–192.

Manner, B. (2001). Learning styles and multiple intelligences in students. *Journal of College Science Teaching, 30,* 390–393.

Martin, R. J., Van Cleaf, D. W., & Hodges, C. A. (1988). Cooperative learning: Linking reading and social studies. *Reading Psychology, 9*(1), 59–72.

Massich, M., & Munoz, E. (1996). Utilizing primary sources as building blocks for literacy. *Social Studies Review, 36*(1), 52–57.

Matanzo, J. B., & Richardson, J. S. (1998). An operatic read-aloud for music and art. *Journal of Adolescent & Adult Literacy, 41,* 490–493.

Mazzoni, S. A., & Gambrell, L. B. (1996). Text talk: Using discussion to promote comprehension of informational texts. In L. B. Gambrell & J. F. Almasi (Eds.), *Lively discussions! Fostering engaged reading* (pp. 134–148). Newark, DE: International Reading Association.

McDonnell, L. M., & McLaughlin, M. J. (1997). *Educating one and all: Students with disabilities and standards-based reform.* Washington, DC: National Academy Press.

McKerrow, K. (1997). Ability grouping: Protecting relative advantage. *Journal for a Just and Caring Education, 3,* 333–342.

McTighe, J., & Wiggins, G. (1999). *The understanding by design handbook.* Alexandria, VA: Association for Supervision and Curriculum Development.

Mehan, H. (1979). *Learning lessons.* Cambridge, MA: Harvard University Press.

Meier, D. (1995). *The power of their ideas: Lessons for America from a small school in Harlem.* Boston: Beacon.

Messaris, P. (1994). *Visual literacy: Image, mind, & reality.* Boulder, CO: Westview.

Miller, T. (1998). The place of picture books in middle-level classrooms. *Journal of Adolescent & Adult Literacy, 41,* 376–381.

Moss, B. (1991). Children's nonfiction trade books: A complement to content-area texts. *The Reading Teacher, 45,* 26–32.

Mundy, J., & Hadaway, N. L. (1999). Children's informational picture books visit a secondary ESL classroom. *Journal of Adolescent & Adult Literacy, 42,* 464–475.

Nagy, W. E., & Anderson, R. C. (1984). How many words are there in printed school English? *Reading Research Quarterly, 19,* 303–330.

National Association of State Boards of Education (NASBE). (1995). *Winning ways: Creating inclusive schools, classrooms, and communities.* Report of the NASBE study group on special education. Washington, DC: Author.

National Association of State Boards of Education (NASBE). (1996). *What will it take? Standards-based education for all students.* Alexandria, VA: Author.

Nezavdal, F. (2003). The standardized testing movement: Equitable or excessive? *McGill Journal of Education, 38,* 65–78.

Nieto, S. (1996). *Affirming diversity: The sociopolitical context of multicultural education* (2nd ed.). White Plains, NY: Longman.

Ogle, D. M. (1986). K-W-L: A teaching model that develops active reading of expository text. *The Reading Teacher, 39,* 564–70.

Onosko, J. J., & Jorgensen, C. M. (1997). Unit and lesson planning in the inclusive classroom: Maximizing learning opportunities for all students. In C. M. Jorgensen (Ed.), *Restructuring high schools for all students: Taking inclusion to the next level* (pp. 71–106). Baltimore, MD: Paul H. Brookes.

Opitz, M. F. (1992). The cooperative reading activity: An alternative to ability grouping. *The Reading Teacher, 45,* 736–738.

Palincsar, A. S., & Brown, A. L. (1986). Interactive teaching to promote independent learning from text. *The Reading Teacher, 39,* 771–777.

Paris, S. G., & Ayres, L. R. (1994). *Becoming reflective students and teachers with portfolios and authentic assessment.* Washington, DC: American Psychological Association.

Perchemlides, N., & Coutant, C. (2004). Growing beyond grades. *Educational Leadership, 62*(2), 53–56.

Perry, N. E. (1998). Young children's self-regulated learning and contexts that support it. *Journal of Educational Psychology, 90,* 715–729.

Peterson, J. S., & Margolin, L. (1997). Naming gifted children: An example of unintended "reproduction." *Journal for the Education of the Gifted, 21*(1), 82–101.

Pokrywcaynski, J. (1992). *War stories can make horror stories: The characteristics students look for in a good advertising guest speaker.* Washington, DC: U.S. Department of Education.

Popham, W. J. (1999). Why standardized tests don't measure educational quality. *Educational Leadership, 56*(6), 8–15.

Posner, G. (1995). *Analyzing the curriculum* (2nd ed.). New York: McGraw-Hill.

Powell, D., & Hornsby, D. (1993). *Learning phonics and spelling in a whole language classroom.* New York: Scholastic Professional Books.

Prain, V., & Hand, B. (1996). Writing for learning in secondary science: Rethinking practices. *Teaching and Teacher Education, 12,* 609–626.

Prawat, R. S. (1999). Dewey, Peirce, and the learning paradox. *American Educational Research Journal, 36,* 47–76.

Raphael, T. E. (1986). Teaching question-answer relationships, revisited. *The Reading Teacher, 39,* 516–522.

Raphael, T. E., Engler, C. S., & Kirschner, B. W. (1986). *The impact of text structure instruction and social context on students' comprehension and production of expository text.* (Research Series No. 177). East Lansing: Michigan State University Institute for Research on Teaching.

Reutzel, D. R. (1999). Organizing literacy instruction: Effective grouping strategies and organizational plans. In L. B. Gambrell, L. M. Morrow, S. B. Neuman, & M. Pressley (Eds.), *Best practices in literacy instruction* (pp. 271–291). New York: Guilford.

Richardson, J. S. (1997–1998). A read-aloud for foreign languages: Becoming a language master. *Journal of Adolescent & Adult Literacy, 41,* 312–314.

Roach, V. (1999). Reflecting on the least restrictive environment policy: Curriculum, instruction, placement—Three legs of the achievement stool. In D. Fisher, C. Sax, & I. Pumpian (Eds.), *Inclusive high schools: Learning from contemporary classrooms* (pp. 145–156). Baltimore, MD: Paul H. Brookes.

Romanowski, M. H. (1996). Problems of bias in history textbooks. *Social Education, 60,* 170–173.

Romero, M. K. (1994). Identifying giftedness among Keresan Pueblo Indians: The Keres study. *Journal of American Indian Education, 34*(1), 35–58.

Ross, E. W. (Ed.). (1997). *The social studies curriculum: Purposes, problems, and possibilities.* Albany, NY: SUNY.

Ruddell, M. R. (1991). Authentic assessment: Focused observation as a means for evaluating language and literacy development. *The California Reader, 24*(2), 2–7.

Ruddell, M. R. (1996). Engaging students' interest and willing participation in subject area learning. In D. Lapp, J. Flood, & N. Farnan (Eds.), *Content area reading and learning: Instructional strategies* (2nd ed., pp. 95–110). Boston: Allyn & Bacon.

Sadker, D. (1999). Gender equity: Still knocking at the door. *Educational Leadership, 56*(7), 22–26.

Santa, C. M., & Havens, L. (1995). *Creating independence through student-owned projects: Project CRISS.* Dubuque, IA: Kendall-Hunt.

Santa, C. M., Havens, L., & Harrison, S. (1996). Teaching secondary science through reading, writing, studying, and problem solving. In D. Lapp, J. Flood, & N. Farnan (Eds.), *Content area reading and learning: Instructional strategies* (2nd ed., pp. 165–179). Boston: Allyn & Bacon.

Sapon-Shevin, M. (1994a). Why gifted students belong in inclusive schools. *Educational Leadership, 52*(4), 64–68, 70.

Sapon-Shevin, M. (1994b). *Playing favorites: Gifted education and the disruption of community.* New York: State University of New York.

Saunders, W. L. (1992). The constructivist perspective: Implications and teaching strategies for science. *School Science and Mathematics, 92*(3), 136–141.

Sautter, R. C. (1994). Who are today's city kids? Beyond the "deficit model." *Cityschools, 1*(1), 6–10.

Schneider, J. J., & Jackson, S. A. W. (2000). Process drama: A special space and place for writing. *The Reading Teacher, 54,* 38–51.

Semali, L. M., & Pailliotet, A. W. (1999). *Intermediality: The teachers' handbook of critical media literacy.* Boulder, CO: Westview.

Shaver, J. P., Davis, O. L., & Helburn, S. M. (1980). An interpretive report on the status of precollege social education based on three NSF funded studies. In *What are the needs in precollege science, mathematics, and social science education? Views from the field* (pp. 3–18). Washington, DC: National Science Foundation.

Sisk, D. A. (1994). Bridging the gap between minority disadvantaged high potential children and Anglo middle class gifted children. *Gifted Education International, 10*(1), 37–43.

Slavin, R. E. (1989). Cooperative learning models for the 3 R's. *Educational Leadership, 47*(4), 22–28.

Slavin, R. E. (1990). *Cooperative learning: Theory, research, practice.* Boston: Allyn & Bacon.

Slavin, R. E. (1995). A model of effective instruction. *Educational Forum, 59*(2), 166–176.

Slavin, R. E. (1996). A cooperative learning approach to content area teaching. In D. Lapp, J. Flood, & N. Farnan (Eds.), *Content area reading and learning: Instructional strategies* (2nd ed., pp. 369–382). Needham Heights, MA: Allyn & Bacon.

Smith-D'Arezzo, W., & Kennedy, B. (2004). Seeing double: Piecing writing together with cross-age partners. *Journal of Adolescent & Adult Literacy, 47,* 390–401.

Soderman, A., Gregory, K. M., & O'Neill, L. T. (1999). *Scaffolding emergent literacy.* Boston: Allyn & Bacon.

Spandel, V., & Stiggins, R. J. (1997). *Creating writers: Linking writing assessment and instruction* (2nd ed.). New York: Longman.

Spear, R. C. (1994). Teachers' perceptions of ability grouping practices in middle level schools. *Research in Middle Level Education, 18,* 117–130.

Spor, M. W., & Schneider, B. K. (1999). Content reading strategies: What teachers know, use, and want to learn. *Reading Research and Instruction, 38,* 221–231.

Squire, J. R. (1987). *Studies of textbooks: Are we asking the right questions?* Paper presented at the Inaugural Conference of the Benton Center for Curriculum and Instruction, University of Chicago.

Stanley, J. C., & Hopkins, K. D. (1972). *Educational and psychological measurement and evaluation.* Englewood Cliffs, NJ: Prentice Hall.

Strom, R. (1990). Talented children in minority families. *International Journal of Early Childhood, 22*(2), 39–48.

Sulzby, E. (1991). Assessment of emergent literacy: Storybook reading. *The Reading Teacher, 44,* 498–500.

Swing, S. R., & Peterson, P. L. (1982). The relationship of student ability and small group interaction to student achievement. *American Educational Research Journal, 19,* 259–274.

Tomlinson, C. A. (1999). *The differentiated classroom: Responding to the needs of all learners.* Alexandria, VA: Association for Supervision and Curriculum Development.

Towell, J. H. (1999–2000). Motivating students through music and literature. *The Reading Teacher, 53,* 284–287.

Trafton, P., Reys, B., & Wasman, D. (2001). Standards-based mathematics curriculum materials: A phrase in search of a definition. *Phi Delta Kappan, 83,* 259–64.

Tucker, M. S., & Codding, J. B. (1998). *Standards for our schools: How to set them, measure them, and reach them.* San Francisco: Jossey-Bass.

Tunnell, M. O., & Ammon, R. (1996). The story of ourselves: Fostering multiple historical perspectives. *Social Education, 57,* 224–225.

Tunseth, J., & Nowicki, C. (2003). The promise of partnerships. *Principal Leadership, 4,* 43–46.

U.S. Department of Education. (1996). *To assure the free appropriate public education of all children with disabilities.* Eighteenth annual report to Congress. Washington, DC: Author.

U.S. Department of Education. (1999). *To assure the free appropriate public education of all children with disabilities (IDEA, Section 618).* Twenty-first annual report to Congress on the implementation of the Individuals with Disabilities Education Act. Washington, DC: Author.

Vacca, R. T., Vacca, J. L., Prosenjak, N., & Burkey, L. (1996). Creating response-centered learning environments. In D. Lapp, J. Flood, & N. Farnan (Eds.), *Content area reading and learning: Instructional strategies* (2nd ed., pp. 355–367). Boston: Allyn & Bacon.

Vygotsky, L. S. (1978). Interaction between learning and development. In M. Cole, V. John-Steiner, S. Scribner, & E. Souberman (Eds. and Trans.), *Mind in society: The development of higher psychological processes* (pp. 79–91). Cambridge, MA: Harvard University Press.

Watts-Taffe, S., & Truscott, D. M. (2000). Using what we know about language and literacy development for ESL students in the mainstream classroom. *Language Arts, 77,* 258–265.

West, G. B. (1978). *Teaching reading skills in content areas: A practical guide to the construction of student exercises* (2nd ed.). Oviedo, FL: Sandpiper.

West, K. R. (1998). Noticing and responding to learners: Literacy evaluation and instruction in the primary grades. *The Reading Teacher, 51,* 550–559.

Wilcox, B. L. (1997). Writing portfolios: Active vs. passive. *English Journal, 86*(6), 34–37.

Wilkinson, L. C., & Silliman, E. R. (2000). Classroom language and literacy learning. In M. L. Kamil, P. B. Mosenthal, P. D. Pearson, & R. Barr (Eds.), *Handbook of reading research: Vol. 3* (pp. 311–335). Mahwah, NJ: Lawrence Erlbaum.

Winograd, P., & Arrington, H. J. (1999). Best practices in literacy assessment. In L. B. Gambrell, L. M. Morrow, S. B. Neumann, & M. Pressley (Eds.), *Best practices in literacy instruction* (pp. 210–241). New York: Guilford.

Winograd, P., & Paris, S. G. (1989). A cognitive and motivational agenda for reading instruction. *Educational Leadership, 46*(4), 30–36.

Woodward, A., Elliott, D. L., & Nagel, K. C. (1986). Beyond textbooks in elementary social studies. *Social Education, 50,* 50–53.

Worthy, J., & Hoffman, J. V. (1996). Critical questions. *The Reading Teacher, 49,* 656–657.

Worthy, J., & Hoffman, J. V. (1999). Critical questions. *The Reading Teacher, 52,* 520–521.

Wortmann, G. B. (1992). An invitation to learning. *Science Teacher, 59*(2), 19–22.

Yancey, K. B. (1992). *Portfolios in the writing classroom.* Urbana, IL: National Council of Teachers of English.

Yell, M. L., Rogers, D., & Rogers, E. L. (1998). The legal history of special education: What a long, strange trip it's been! *Remedial and Special Education, 19,* 219–228.

Zunino, B., & Hill, G. (2003). Changing the image of an inner-city school. *Education, 123,* 428–431.

CHILDREN'S LITERATURE CITED

Adler, D. (1995). *A picture book of Rosa Parks*. New York: Holiday House.

Artman, J. (1987). *Pioneers*. New York: Good Apple.

Boas, J. (1996). *We are witnesses: Five diaries of teenagers who died in the Holocaust*. New York: Scholastic.

Cerebellum Corporation. (2002). *Standard deviants school physics companion* [DVD]. Falls Church, VA.

Coerr, E. (1999). *Sadako*. New York: Puffin.

Cole, J. (1996). *The magic school bus blows its top*. New York: Scholastic.

Cushman, K. (1995). *Catherine, called Birdy*. New York: Harper Trophy.

Cushman, K. (2000). *Matilda bone*. New York: Clarion.

David, R. (1993). *Growing up in ancient Egypt*. Mahwah, NJ: Troll.

De Angeli, M. (1990). *The door in the wall*. New York: Yearling.

Denenberg, B. (1997). *Voices from Vietnam*. New York: Scholastic.

Dodds, D. A. (1989). *Wheel away*. New York: Scholastic.

Douglass, F. (1994). *Escape from slavery: The boyhood of Frederick Douglass in his own words*. New York: Knopf.

Filipovic, Z. (1995). *Zlata's diary : A child's life in Sarajevo*. New York: Penguin.

Fleischman, P. (1988). *Joyful noise: Poems for two voices*. New York: Harper-Collins.

Fradin, D. (1984). *Explorers*. New York: Children's Press.

Frank, A., & Mooyaart, B. M. (1993). *Anne Frank: The diary of a young girl*. New York: Bantam.

Garland, S. (1995). *The silent storm*. New York: Harcourt Brace.

Garland, S. (1997). *The lotus seed*. New York: Voyager.

Giblin, J. (2000). *The amazing life of Benjamin Franklin*. New York: Scholastic.

Gollub, M. (1998). *Cool melons-turn to frogs! The life and poems of Issa*. New York: Lee & Low.

Hauser, J. F. (1999). *Gizmos and gadgets: Creating science contraptions that work*. Charlotte, VT: Williamson.

Heard, G. (2002). *This place I know: Poems of comfort*. Cambridge, MA: Candlewick Press.

Huynh, S. T. (1996). *An anthology of Vietnamese poems: From the eleventh through the twentieth centuries*. New Haven, CT: Yale.

Ianzelo, T., & Low, C. (Producers). (2002). *Momentum* [Motion Picture]. Chatsworth, CA: Image Entertainment.

Jimenez, F. (1996). *The circuit*. New York: Houghton Mifflin.

Knight, M. B. (1993). *Who belongs here? An American story*. Gardiner, ME: Tilbury.

Kodama, T. (1995). *Shin's tricycle*. New York: Walker.

Kramer, S. (1997). *Eye of the storm: Chasing storms with Warren Faidley*. New York: Putnam.

Krull, K. (1993). *Lives of the musicians: Good times, bad times (and what the neighbors thought)*. San Diego, CA: Harcourt Brace.

Langley, A., Dann, G., & Brightling, G. (2000). *Eyewitness: Medieval life*. New York: DK Publishing.

Lauber, P. (1999). *What you never knew about fingers, forks, and chopsticks*. New York: Alladin.

Lowry, L. (1989). *Number the stars*. New York: Houghton Mifflin.

MacDonald, F. (1997). *How would you survive in the Middle Ages?* New York: Franklin Watts.

MacDonald, F. (1999). *Women in ancient Egypt: The other half of history*. Lincolnwood, IL: Peter Bedrick.

McKay, L. (1998). *Journey home*. New York: Lee & Low.

Moerbeek, K., & Dijs, C. (1997). *Six brave explorers: A pop-up book*. Pensacola, FL: Presto Print.

Montgomery, J., & Hinson, M. (1995). *Meet the great composers*. Van Nuys, CA: Alfred.

Pappas, T. (1991). *Math talk: Mathematical ideas in poems for two voices*. San Carlos, CA: World Wide Publishing/Tetra.

Paulsen, G. (1999). *My life in dog years*. New York: Yearling.

Pinkney, A. D. (1998). *Dear Benjamin Banneker*. New York: Voyager.

Prelutsky, J. (1996). *Pizza the size of the sun: Poems by Jack Prelutsky*. New York: Greenwillow.

Pyle, H. (1967). *Otto of the silver hand*. Mineola, NY: Dover.

Rappaport, D. (2001). *Martin's big words: The life of Martin Luther King, Jr.*. New York: Jump at the Sun.

Rice, E. (2000). *Life during the Middle Ages: The way people live*. New York: Lucent.

Robertson, B. (1999). *Marguerite makes a book*. Los Angeles: J. Paul Getty Museum.

Roop, C. (1999). *Girl of the shining mountains: Sacagawea's story*. New York: Hyperion.

Sandburg, C. (1995). *Poetry for young people*. New York: Sterling.

Shepard, A. (1998). *The crystal heart: A Vietnamese legend*. New York: Atheneum.

Sis, P. (1996). *Follow the dream*. New York: Dragonfly.

Soto, G. (1996). *Canto familiar*. San Diego, CA: Harcourt Brace.

Spinelli, J. (1998). *Knots in my yo-yo string: The autobiography of a kid*. New York: Knopf.

Spivak, D. (1997). *Grass sandals: The travels of Basho*. New York: Atheneum.

Steinbeck, J. (1937). *Of mice and men*. New York: Penguin.

Stewart, A. (2000). *Keeping clean: Everyday history*. New York: Franklin Watts.

Surat, M. S. (1989). *Angel child, dragon child*. New York: Scholastic.

Tanaka, S. (1996). *Anastasia's album*. New York: Hyperion.

Uchida, Y. (1995). *The invisible thread: An autobiography*. Sussex, UK: Beech Tree.

VanCleave, J. (1991). *Janice VanCleave's physics for every kid: 101 easy experiments in motion, heat, light, machines, and sound*. Hoboken, NJ: Wiley.

Vining, E. G. (1987). *Adam of the road*. New York: Viking.

Whelan, G. (1993). *Goodbye, Vietnam*. New York: Random House.

White, E. B. (1974). *Charlotte's web*. New York: HarperTrophy.

Winter, J. (1999). *Sebastian: A book about Bach*. San Diego, CA: Harcourt Brace.

ABOUT THE AUTHORS

Nancy Frey, **Douglas Fisher**, and **Kelly Moore** are faculty members in teacher education at San Diego State University and coordinate the professional development school efforts of several elementary and secondary schools. They are interested in urban education, student achievement, and planning curriculum and instruction for all students.